A Personal Year of Grace

Spiritual Growth Through the Liturgical Year

Warren Dicharry, C.M.

A Liturgical Press Book

THE LITURGICAL PRESS
Collegeville, Minnesota

Cover design by Greg Becker.

1   2   3   4   5   6   7   8   9

Library of Congress Cataloging-in-Publication Data

Dicharry, Warren F.
    A personal year of grace : spiritual growth through the liturgical year / Warren F. Dicharry.
        p.   cm.
    ISBN 0-8146-2221-6
    1. Spiritual life—Catholic Church. 2. Church year. 3. Catholic Church—Doctrines. I. Title.
    BX2350.2.D494   1996
    263'.9—dc20   95-13676
                                                                                       CIP

To all who feel themselves called
to follow and attain Christ Jesus,
this work is cordially dedicated.

CONTENTS

INTRODUCTION

Until about four years ago, the Church year had meant precisely that to me—the year of the Church. As such, I had been faithful in celebrating it annually. But the Church is made up of individual persons, of whom I happen to be one. And so I began to wonder what it would be like to regard the Church year as a year of personal spiritual growth. The results have been nothing short of electrifying. I have written this little book containing the main elements of my experience. If my readers will read it, apply it to themselves personally, and remain prayerfully open to whatever the Lord desires to work within them, I feel certain that they will obtain results that go far beyond their expectations. If this little volume contributes anything at all toward that end, I will feel amply justified and ask for nothing more.

I am frankly appalled by how few books there are on this subject. The vast majority of books on the Church year treat of how it came about. However, since my concern is with the liturgical year as it stands today and as it affects our personal spiritual life, I will omit most references to its historical development.

In no way do I deny the collective nature of the Church year. Neither am I suggesting that the personal approach to the liturgical year is the only, or even the best, one possible. All I am saying is that—besides the communitarian attitude which has taken so long to inculcate—there is another one available and that it ought to be tried.

I have taken all my Scripture quotations from the current revised edition of the New American Bible without any personal translations such as I have done in former books, because this particular volume is not meant to be a scholarly work and therefore does not require a precise knowledge of the original language.

Warren F. Dicharry, C.M.

1 PERSONAL SPIRITUAL GROWTH THROUGH THE CHURCH YEAR

Since the Church community is made up of individual persons and since sanctification and salvation are personal achievements, albeit through cooperation with God's grace, our concern in this work is entirely with the personal. In this treatment, we are demanding nothing more and nothing less than total honesty with God and with ourselves as required by the very nature of the person.

"Spiritual" here refers to that deepest part of our being where we encounter God: "The Spirit itself bears witness with our spirit that we are children of God" (Rom 8:16). In the description of our nature (Gen 2:7), spirit is that dimension of our being—represented by the Hebrew *rhuah* and the Greek *pneûma*—whereby we are always aspiring to union with God. By contrast, as flesh (Hebrew *bashar*, Greek *sárx*), we are constantly liable to illness, injury, and death as well as to temptation and sin. Throughout our lives, as Paul makes abundantly clear in Galatians 5 and Romans 8, we as persons (Hebrew *nefesh*, Greek *psyché* or *sôma*) are involved in a lifelong struggle between spirit and flesh. This is not a struggle between body and soul, as we are inclined to view it from our Greek philosophical background, but rather between our *whole being* aspiring to union with God and our *whole being* inclined to temptation and sin.

I prefer to call the entire realm of the spiritual, the "spiritual life" rather than "spirituality" in order to emphasize that this is not an abstraction but rather a life, the risen life of Christ himself, that we are called upon to live. Again returning to Genesis for our origin, but this time to Genesis 1:26-27, we read, "Then God said: 'Let us make man in our image, after

1

our likeness. . . .' God created man in his image; in the divine image he created him; male and female he created them.'' Now, besides the literal meanings of dominance and sexuality that seem to lie here because of the immediate context, I think that there is also a spiritual meaning made clear in Romans 8:29: ''For those he foreknew he also predestined to be conformed to the image of his Son. . . .'' In other words, what God had intended from the beginning was brought about through the incarnation, death, and resurrection of his dearly beloved Son, Jesus Christ.

Jesus was born, lived, and died for us; then he rose from the dead and, in his risen form, has continued to live among us and within us, insofar as we permit him to do so. Each of us is utterly unique. There will never be another you or another me. And Jesus, the risen Christ, desires to take possession of us, with our freely given consent, so that he can see with our eyes, listen with our ears, speak with our tongue, think with our mind, love with our heart, work with our hands, yes, and suffer with our body. Does Paul not say in Colossians 1:24, ''. . . and in my flesh I am filling up what is lacking in the afflictions of Christ on behalf of his body, which is the church. . . .'' How can anything be lacking in the afflictions of Christ except in the sense that, in his risen state, he can continue to live and to suffer in and through us? What Christ desires of us, then, is what I propose he brings about, not only through his Church and sacraments, not only through prayer and service, but also through the Church year.

Growth is something essential to us. At a time when the Church was extremely conservative, the time of Vatican I (1869–70), the great Cardinal Newman was declaring that ''to live is to change, and to be perfect is to have changed often.''[1] And again, along the same line, ''Growth is the only proof of life.''[2] In the spiritual life especially, not to go forward is to go backward, not to grow forward is to grow backward. The

1. John Henry Newman, ''Development of Christian Doctrine,'' *Newman's Apologia: A Classic Reconsidered,* ed. Vincent Blehl and Francis Connolly (New York: Harcourt, Brace & World, 1964) 139.

2. John Henry Newman, *Apologia pro Vita Sua: Being a History of His Religious Opinions* (New York: Longmans, Green & Co., 1947) 5.

author presumes that the readers of this little work are people who, with all of their ability, truly desire personal spiritual growth in the Lord.

The question is how to achieve this personal spiritual growth in the Lord. The answer lies in that little parable which is unique to Mark's gospel:

> He said, "This is how it is with the kingdom of God; it is as if a man were to scatter seed on the land and would sleep and rise night and day and the seed would sprout and grow, he knows not how. Of its own accord the land yields fruit, first the blade, then the ear, then the full grain in the ear. And when the grain is ripe, he wields the sickle at once, for the harvest has come" (4:26-29).

The secret lies in the realm of nature, in the growth of the seed, which Jesus himself explains: "The seed is the word of God" (Luke 8:11). Now the word of God may be understood in two senses—as the word about God or his kingdom, which seems to be the primary meaning of the parable of the sower; or as the Incarnate Word of God, the Word who "became flesh" (John 1:14) and forms the primary meaning of the prologue to John's Gospel, or the beginning of John's First Letter, and of Revelation 19:13. In the great Letter to the Hebrews, the expression "the word of God" seems to refer to both meanings. In Hebrews 4:12-13, Paul says:

> Indeed, the word of God is living and effective, sharper than any two-edged sword, penetrating even between soul and spirit, joints and marrow, and able to discern reflections and thoughts of the heart. No creature is concealed from him, but everything is naked and exposed to the eyes of him to whom we must render an account.

But what is the difference between this extensive use of "the Word of God" throughout the liturgical year from a similar use of natural imagery in the nature religions of ancient Greece, for example in the Eleusinian mysteries. The difference is simple, of course: it is between what was based on the real life, birth, death, and resurrection of Jesus Christ, "the Word of God," and what was only legendary, drawn from the natural cycle of the growth of grain.

Having indicated what it is that we are primarily concerned with—namely, personal spiritual growth—let us now turn to the liturgical year of the Church to see how the two come together.

Having spoken of personal spiritual growth, it remains for us to see how this can be accomplished through the Church year, relying heavily on an understanding of sacred liturgy which is perhaps not treated sufficiently. Liturgy is not primarily for celebrating the past mysteries of the Incarnate Word; it makes present for us today what, through sacred Scripture, we know of as the mysteries of Christ so that we can play our important role in them. In Romans 12:1-2, we read:

> I urge you therefore, brothers, by the mercies of God, to offer your bodies as a living sacrifice, holy and pleasing to God, your spiritual worship. Do not conform yourself to this age but be transformed by the renewal of your mind, that you may discern what is the will of God, what is good and pleasing and perfect.

This note of presentation is confirmed by the Second Vatican Council in its great *Constitution on the Sacred Liturgy*, which was the very first document promulgated. After treating the deeds of Jesus in working out our redemption, this document then states in *Sacrosanctum Concilium*, Introduction, paragraph 6 and 7:

> From that time onward the Church has never failed to come together to celebrate the paschal mystery, reading those things "which were in all the scriptures concerning him" (Luke 24:27), celebrating the Eucharist in which "the victory and triumph of his death are again made present," and at the same time "giving thanks to God for his inexpressible gift" (2 Cor 9:15) in Christ Jesus, "in praise of his glory" (Eph 1:12) through the power of the Holy Spirit. To accomplish so great a work, Christ is always present in his Church, especially in her liturgical celebrations. He is present in the Sacrifice of the Mass not only in the person of his minister, "the same now offering, through the ministry of priests, who formerly offered himself on the cross," but especially in the Eucharistic species. By his power he is present in the sacraments so that when anybody baptizes it is really Christ him-

self who baptizes. He is present in his Word since it is he himself who speaks when the holy Scriptures are read in the Church. Lastly, he is present when the Church prays and sings, for he has promised "where two or three are gathered together in my name there am I in the midst of them" (Matt 18:20).

And in Chapter V, "The Liturgical Year," we read in paragraph 102:

> Thus recalling the mysteries of the redemption, she opens up to the faithful the riches of her Lord's powers and merits, so that these are in some way made present for all time: the faithful lay hold of them and are filled with saving grace.

In summary, then, the liturgy makes present what we learn from sacred Scripture so that we, the followers of Christ, may join him in his paschal mysteries. But how is this done in the case of the Church's year? That is the question now before us. Perhaps we can deal with this subject best by dividing it into three sections. In the first section, the Christmas cycle, we will consider the Word of God as longing to be implanted in us in a new way. So, during the Advent season, the season of preparation, we will plow and harrow the land, especially through the help of Mary, the Virgin Mother of Jesus, two of whose feasts we celebrate during this time. Then, during the Christmas cycle properly so-called, including the great feasts of the Holy Family (Sunday after Christmas) and the Divine Maternity (January 1), we will plumb the meaning of this great feast of Christmas, especially as it involves the implantation anew in us of the Word of God.

Then, with the feast of the Epiphany (Manifestation) followed by the brief period of Ordinary time I, we will have the opportunity to consider the beginnings of growth within us of the Word of God.

Now comes the Easter cycle, with Lent forming a period of weeding out and pruning prior to the great mysteries of Christ in the Easter Triduum, when we celebrate the blossoming, the blooming within us of the Word of God. We must not forget that there will only be as much fruit at the end of the year as there are blossoms at Easter. This marvelous period of blooming goes on until Pentecost with the coming anew of the Holy Spirit to transform us into Christ.

The entire second half of the Church year is occupied by Ordinary Time II, but this should be expected because in nature it takes time for things to grow and ripen. All during the hot summer when the Scripture readings are about the Holy Eucharist, we endure and celebrate the feasts of the Holy Trinity, Corpus Christi, and the Sacred Heart of Jesus; then, later in the summer, we look to the Assumption, and into the fall, with its feasts of All Saints and All Souls, finally conclude the Church year with the great feast of Christ the King. We hope that we will be much closer to Christ, the King of our hearts, by this feast than we were at the beginning of the Church year.

This may seem trite and commonplace when we summarize the Church's year like this, but when we get into it and are more fully concerned with each part, it will seem otherwise. Perhaps it would have been better not to have given this brief summary. That is difficult to determine; we shall simply have to trust God as well as the critical sense of our readers.

But in the concrete, just how are we affected by these moments in the Church year? We can answer this in three ways: through the Eucharistic sacrifice of the Mass, through the liturgical hours of the Breviary, and through our own personal prayer life. Let us look briefly at each one of these three.

First, I have long since learned to regard *the Eucharist as a beautiful drama* in which the Church has surrounded the original act of Jesus (which would have taken less than a minute) with additional words, prayers, scripture readings, gestures, song, sometimes even dance, all done in the special costume and color of the day, all for the purpose of helping us to appreciate what is happening. And, in case there are people who are turned off by the suggestion of the Mass as a drama, let me quickly remind them that, historically speaking, today's drama collection is an outgrowth of the excellent mystery and miracle plays of the Church in the Middle Ages.

Now, in a drama, there are acts and scenes. So, in the drama of the Eucharist, there are two acts known to us as the liturgy of the Word and the liturgy of the Eucharist, each with its own scenes. In the liturgy of the Word, we have two scenes in which we first address the Father, expressing sorrow for our sins, glorifying him in that beautiful hymn which begins with the song of the angels at Bethlehem, and then gathering the collected prayers of the faithful together in what we call the collect. Then God in his turn speaks to us in the second scene from the Old Testament (with a responsorial psalm), the New Testament, the gospel, and the homily. Thus we have a beautiful dialogue of love and life in word and in tongue. But as St. John tells us in 1 John 3:18, "Children, let us love not in word or speech but in deed and truth." And that is what we are about to do in the liturgy of the Eucharist. But before leaving the liturgy of the Word, let me point out that, since Vatican II, the liturgy of the Word has taken its proper place so that, for example, the faithful are no longer told that they must be in church for the presentation of the gifts in order to have heard Mass. The entire Mass is important now, and the Church has wisely spread the Scriptures over a three-year cycle so that most of them will be covered with no danger of loss or boredom.

Before entering into the liturgy of the Eucharist, at least on Sundays and solemnities, we recite the Creed or profession of faith in order to stir up our faith because, without faith, the liturgy of the Eucharist is meaningless. In the liturgy of the Eucharist, there are three main scenes, each one important in itself. First comes the presentation of the gifts, the offering of bread and wine to God Our Father. But we are not just offering bread and wine, we are offering ourselves. The bread and wine represent us—all that we are, have, do, and suffer. We are clearly reminded of this both by the summary of Azariah's prayer in Daniel 3:38-40 which the priest says immediately after offering the wine and before washing his hands, as well as by his request to pray that our sacrifice may be acceptable to God, our almighty Father.

In the second scene we come to the heart of the Mass, the changing of bread and wine into the body and blood of Christ by the repetition of the Words of institution found in 1 Corinthians 11:23-26, Matthew 26:26-29, Mark 14:22-25, and Luke 22:19-20. One of the more remarkable things brought out in the original Greek passages is that all of them are in the present tense. In other words, for all ages the time of the Eucharist is the present. Bear in mind that the bread and wine represent us, so we are ourselves being changed more and more into Christ with each celebration of the Eucharist. If we were free of any selfish thoughts, words, and deeds, it would take only one Eucharist to transform us into Christ, but we have gathered such a backlog of rubbish over the years that it may take us years before we are transformed, if we ever are.

The final scene of the Eucharist is the reception of Communion which begins with the Lord's Prayer. Having offered ourselves with Christ to the Father, now the Father returns the favor and gives us the Son to eat. This is also a great means of conversion. As we have learned from nutritionists these days, we are what we eat. So, as we receive the Lord in Holy Communion, we become more and more Christ. And since we all receive the same bread and wine, we become more and more a united group; therefore, as a result of the Eucharist, we should be "of one heart and mind" (Acts 4:32).

After the Communion, there is a brief moment for thanksgiving, then the final prayer, blessing, and dismissal, all of which remind us that we go forth from the church or chapel filled with Christ and ready to witness to him to all whom we encounter. We are no longer merely human, but possessed now of and by Christ.

In writing about the Holy Eucharist, I am well aware of the fact that I have considered only the personal effects involved without treating its role as the sacrifice of the Church or its role as a covenant sacrifice. It is not that I think less of its communitarian or covenant roles, but that I have chosen to underline its personal role in keeping with the theme of personal spiritual growth.

Now, in treating the liturgical hours, developed in the Church "to sanctify the day" (*Sacrosanctum Concilium*, par. 88), our concern will embrace both the communal and personal. Priests, deacons, religious, and an increasing number of lay people

> will pray the divine office the more fervently, the more alive they are to the need to heed St. Paul's exhortation, "Pray without ceasing" (1 Thess 5:17). For only the Lord who said, "Without me you can do nothing," can make their work more effective and fruitful. That is why the apostles when

instituting deacons said, ''We will devote ourselves to prayer and to the ministry of the word'' (Acts 6:4) (*Sacrosanctum Concilium*, par. 86).

Therefore, when this wonderful song of praise is correctly celebrated by priests and others deputed to it by the Church, or by the faithful praying together with a priest in the approved form, then it is truly the voice of the Bride herself addressed to her Bridegroom. It is the very prayer which Christ himself together with his Body addresses to the Father (*Sacrosanctum Concilium*, par. 84).

After such sublime words, who can refuse to say the Office? Yet I am well aware that there are priests who have not said a word of the liturgical hours in years, using as their excuse that their jobs are too demanding. If they are too busy to pray, they are too busy. If they would only recite the Hours daily, they would quickly find that their excuse is foolish indeed. What I personally have found over the years is that it is largely a question of spreading the Office over the day, sanctifying the day according to the original intention.

Thus, I say lauds with the community in the morning, one of the little hours after breakfast, vespers after lunch, and the hour of readings later in the afternoon, with compline being said after supper. In fact, lately I have even said the Office when traveling, reciting lauds and little hours in the morning before leaving, and vespers, the hour of reading, and compline when I have arrived at my destination.

Thus, if one is faithful in saying the liturgical hours, then one is always in tune with Christ and the Church at any given time in the Church's year. For there is no substitute for what one gains daily from the psalms, prayers, and readings which have been so marvelously compiled in four volumes to follow the liturgical year.

Now, we come to our private and *personal prayer life*. I will not dwell long on it because the subject of prayer could easily consume the major part of this little work. Suffice it to say that we need to set aside a definite time each day for personal prayer. A priest, deacon, religious, or dedicated lay person can do no less. Next, let our prayer reflect the season of the year, for those who are easily distracted, the Bible used as a prayer book in what is known as *Lectio Divina* will be useful. But whether we are in meditation, active contemplation, or passive contemplation (all of which are possible for a busy priest or anyone else who seeks God); whether we are in the purgative, illuminative, or unitive way; we need only reflect the liturgical year in our prayer life to derive the enormous fruits thereof.

But what if we encounter only endless darkness, deserts, distractions? Then we need to examine ourselves to see whether they are the result of our way of life or not. If they result from our careless way of life, then we need to make some changes. But if, as is possible, they are the necessary dark night or desert which must take place before we can arrive at a higher form of prayer, then let us continue on toward the light at the end of the tunnel. It all depends on whether or not we are serious about our prayer life.

2 THE CHRISTMAS CYCLE

Now, having seen how the liturgical year pertains to our personal spiritual growth, we begin a study of each part of the Church's year—the Christmas cycle, the Easter cycle, and Ordinary Time—in order to discern there just how we are to live.

Season of Advent

Advent is the beginning of the liturgical year, the time of preparation for the coming of Christ at Christmas and a season of longing for the coming of the Messiah into our hearts and homes. Since it is the beginning of the liturgical year, it should mark the beginning of a new period of grace for us personally. As in any endeavor, we must first make plans, set goals, and arrive at objectives. So should it be at the beginning of Advent. Advent, then, rather than the secular or civil new year, should be the time of our own new year's resolutions. With a view to our own personal spiritual growth, each liturgical year should have its own plans, goals, and objectives. These need not be cumbersome or even carefully written out, but they should be there in our mind and heart at the beginning of the Church year, the opening day of Advent.

Next, Advent is a time of preparation for Christmas. In much the same way as the ground is prepared by plowing and harrowing it in preparation for a new planting, Christmas will mark a new planting of the seed in our hearts, the seed being the Incarnate Word of God. In order for us to prepare ourselves as perfectly as possible, the Church gives us two models, two special feasts which we celebrate during Advent: the feast of the Immaculate Conception of Mary and the feast of Our Lady of Guadalupe on the eighth and twelfth of December, respectively. It is significant that both of the feasts take their gospels

11

from the Gospel of Luke. The feast of the Immaculate Conception uses the annunciation account (Luke 1:25-38); the feast of Our Lady of Guadalupe uses that which follows immediately after, namely, the visitation account (Luke 1:39-47). Let us look at both of those in turn.

A careful study of the annunciation reveals that there is a threefold announcement by the archangel Gabriel and a threefold response by Mary. We will study Gabriel's announcements later, but let us gently and lovingly examine Mary's responses. Her first response is one of humility: she was "greatly troubled at what was said, and pondered what sort of greeting this might be" (Luke 1:29). Her second response is one of purity: "How can this be, since I have no relations with a man?" (Luke 1:34). Her third response is one of complete love: "Behold, I am the handmaid of the Lord. May it be done to me according to your word" (Luke 1:38). From these three responses, it is easy to see that, above all, the ways in which we are to prepare for the coming of the Christ Child at Christmas are simply by humility, purity according to our state in life, and generous love.

Now these virtues are not at all easy to acquire. Humility is the moderator of our instinct for self-preservation. Purity moderates our instinct to perpetuate the human species. Total self-giving love controls our innate sloth and selfishness. An entire lifetime would not suffice even to approach the virtues of "our tainted nature's solitary boast,"[1] but God wants us to continue trying, especially through his all-achieving grace. We can be sure that, for every degree of improvement gained, we are that much better prepared for the implanting of God's Word at Christmas.

The feast of Our Lady of Guadalupe is also very helpful. First of all, in her picture on the *tilma* of Juan Diego, Mary is depicted wearing a typical maternity dress, reminding us that she is expecting the Christ Child. Then, the visitation account contains two main lessons. The first one, Mary's selfless concern for

---

1. William Wordsworth, "The Virgin," *The Poems of William Wordsworth*, ed. John Hayden (New Haven, Conn.: Yale University Press, 1981) 2:474.

her cousin Elizabeth reminds us that our own love must look toward the needs of others. The second lesson, through a whole series of references to chapter six of Second Samuel, shows that Mary is the ark of the covenant of the New Testament. After the untimely death of Uzzah, David exclaims, "How can the ark of the Lord come to me?" (2 Sam 6:9); so he has the ark diverted to the house of Obededom for three months (2 Sam 6:10-11). Then, seeing that the presence of the ark greatly blessed the house of Obededom, he had the ark brought into Jerusalem, welcoming it while leaping and dancing with joy (2 Sam 6:14-16). In the visitation account, Elizabeth cries out, "And how does this happen to me, that the mother of my Lord should come to me?" (Luke 1:43). But Elizabeth welcomes Mary while the child joyfully "leaped in her womb" (Luke 1:41). After her *Magnificat*, "Mary remained with her about three months" (Luke 1:56). Nor is this an isolated instance. In preparation for the vision of the "woman clothed with the sun" (Rev 12:1), "God's temple in heaven was opened, and the ark of his covenant could be seen in the temple" (Rev 11:19).

What is significant about the symbolism of Mary as ark of the covenant is that the covenant, an agreement establishing a bond of relationship between peoples or persons, was the end for which the Law was the means. This can clearly be seen in Exodus 19:3-8 where God, through Moses, invites the Jewish people into a covenant relationship, without any mention of commandments. God only gives Moses the Ten Commandments, afterward, in the following chapter. Around 750 B.C. with the prophet Hosea, the covenant between Yahweh and Israel came to be described in terms of a marriage. In the New Testament, on the night before his death, Jesus establishes the new covenant in his blood at the institution of the Holy Eucharist. In his First Letter, St. Peter makes it clear that, through baptism, we receive the same benefits promised to Israel. In 1 Peter 2:9 he says, "But you are 'a chosen race, a royal priesthood, a holy nation, a people of his own. . . .'" Just as the old ark of the covenant contained some souvenirs of God's goodness such as the tablets of the Law, Mary as the ark of the covenant of the New Testament, contains Christ.

Thirdly and finally, Advent is a season of longing for the coming of the Messiah into our hearts and homes. In a true sense, it represents the many centuries of Old Testament expectations for the coming of the Blessed One. The liturgy of Advent is flooded with a stream of Old Testament prophecy: especially Isaiah 7, 9, and 11, as well as Second Isaiah (Isa 40–66), written some 150 years later out of Babylonian exile. Thus we are asked to identify ourselves with the Jewish people who had for so long awaited their Messiah. It is good for us to do so. For only to the extent that we identify ourselves with the many centuries of Israel's hope and expectations will we be able to begin to appreciate God's loving and totally unexpected answer to those expectations. Most of the Jews were expecting a national, political, military figure who would throw over the Jews' yoke of submission to foreign powers. And what did God send? He sent his own Son to die for us in order to free us from slavery to sin, a totally unexpected and indescribable gift.

As we shall see, it is only if we have spent a good Advent imitating Mary's special virtues of humility, purity, and generous love and identifying ourselves with the centuries of Jews sighing and longing for a Messiah that we will be able to appreciate his coming to us at Christmas. To help us in this regard, the Church provides in Advent (as in Lent) a whole series of mixed Scripture readings which she then invites us to meditate on or contemplate according to our state of spiritual life. If we are faithful, daily using these Scripture readings as intended, then we will indeed be ready for the coming of the Christ Child at Christmas.

To make our Advent preparation more significant, let me end our season of Advent with a song about the meaning of Christmas which I composed a few years ago:

The Meaning of Christmas

They say there will be Santa Claus
As long as there is love.
So let us welcome Santa Claus
Gift-bringing from above.
But Santa's just a symbol of
The One who's over all:

The God of Love who's born for us
    So helpless and so small.
''C'' is for the Christ-Child,
    Sleeping in the hay,
''H'' is for the Heavens,
    Praising God today.
''R'' is for the Rapture
    On his Mother's face.
''I'' is for the Inn too full
    To offer him a place.
''S'' is for the Shining Star
    That guides the Wise Men there.
''T'' is for their Treasures three:
    Incense, gold, and myrrh so rare.
''M'' is for the Manger
    Where he rests his head.
''A'' is for the Angels
    Crowding 'round his bed.
''S'' is for our Savior,
    Bringing Gifts to earth:
Gifts of love and life and light
    That give us all new worth.
On this hushed and holiest night,
    We celebrate his birth;
On this great and glorious night,
    We find our own rebirth.

Christmas

Christmas Day is extremely rich, containing three separate Masses and an additional vigil Mass for the evening before. Let us look at each of these liturgies in order to appreciate what they contain. The vigil liturgy emphasizes the covenant in the first reading and the responsorial psalm. Then, in the middle reading, we have a selection from Paul's first discourse on Jesus given at Antioch in Pisidia. Finally, a part of Matthew's Gospel traces Jesus' descent from Abraham, along with a brief account of his birth from the viewpoint of Joseph.

The liturgy of Christmas midnight Mass contains, in the first reading, the messianic prophecy from the ninth chapter of the Book of Isaiah, verse five:

> For a child is born to us, a son is given us;
> upon his shoulder dominion rests.
> They name him Wonder-Counselor, God-Hero,
> Father-Forever, Prince of Peace.

The responsorial psalm is a selection from a coronation psalm, Psalm 96. The second reading is taken from Titus 2:11-14. And the gospel is nothing less than the account itself of Jesus' birth according to Luke 2:1-14, which is already sufficiently known to us.

The next Mass, which is listed for dawn, begins with a short selection from Isaiah 62:11-12 about the benefits to the Church: "They shall be called the holy people, the redeemed of the Lord, And you shall be called 'Frequented,' a city that is not forsaken." The responsorial psalm is from Psalm 97, another coronation psalm, with special emphasis on Christ as the Light of the World. The second reading is again from Titus concerning the "kindness and love of God" as well as his compassion in redeeming us. And the gospel contains an account of the shepherds' visit to the Christ Child taken from Luke 2:15-20.

Finally, the Mass during the day contains, for its first reading, an excerpt from Isaiah 52:7-10: "How beautiful upon the mountains are the feet of him who brings glad tidings [good news!], announcing peace, bearing good news, announcing salvation, and saying to Zion, 'Your God is King!' " The responsorial psalm is again one of the coronation psalms, Psalm 98. The second reading is the beautiful passage from the beginning of the Epistle to the Hebrews, 1:1-6. Finally, the gospel is the prologue to John's Gospel, full of meaning, so that we may contemplate the divinity of this newborn child at Bethlehem.

But just who is this child who has been born? There are three ways to arrive at an answer to that question: one, by listening carefully to the words of the angel in the annunciation; two, by examining the meaning of the prologue to John's Gospel; and three, by contemplating Paul's teaching on humility in Philippians 2:5-11. Let us examine each of these in turn:

> In the sixth month, the angel Gabriel was sent from God to
> a town of Galilee called Nazareth, to a virgin betrothed to

> a man named Joseph, of the house of David, and the vir-
> gin's name was Mary. And coming to her, he said, "Hail,
> favored one! The Lord is with you" (Luke 1:26-28).

What a model of economy of words and accuracy of details.
Time, the name of the messenger, where from, where to, spe-
cifically to whom, her condition, her name, all are divulged
in one sentence. Then, in another sentence, we have the beginning of Gabriel's message; "Hail" is rather "Rejoice" and
recalls the opening lines of two Messianic prophecies of the
Old Testament, Zephaniah 3:14-20 and Zechariah 9:9-11. Then,
in his next words, "The Lord is with you," he repeats the
words with which God was wont to indicate his special presence with his people, as for example in the call of Gideon in
Judges 6:12.

After Mary's humble response, the angel reveals in detail
the purpose of his mission:

> Do not be afraid, Mary, for you have found favor with God.
> Behold, you will conceive in your womb and bear a son, and
> you shall name him Jesus (Luke 1:30-31).

This is a clear allusion to the famous Emmanuel prophecy in
Isaiah 7:14—with a change from Emmanuel to Jesus—because
Luke's work is designed to portray Jesus as the savior of all
people. After which, the angel continues by alluding first to
the coronation psalms and then to the famous prophecy of
David in 2 Samuel 7:14:

> Behold, you will conceive in your womb and bear a son, and
> you shall name him Jesus. He will be great and will be called
> Son of the Most High, and the Lord God will give him the
> throne of David his father, and he will rule over the house
> of Jacob forever, and of his kingdom there will be no end
> (Luke 1:31-33).

After Mary's second response, one of purity, the angel continues in words reminiscent of the first chapter of Genesis as
well as Exodus 40 since the verb *episkiázo* (overshadow) is the
Septuagint translation of the Hebrew *shakan* in Exodus 40:35
and, elsewhere, its noun form *shekina* refers to the luminous

cloud hovering over the tabernacle in the desert. There is also a play on words, for the noun *to hágion* usually translated "the child" can also mean "the holy place, the temple" as is brought out in John 1:14 and 2:19-21. Finally, he confides to Mary the extraordinary pregnancy of Elizabeth, Mary's cousin:

> The Holy Spirit will come upon you, and the power of the Most High will overshadow you. Therefore the child to be born will be called holy, the Son of God. And behold, Elizabeth, your relative, has also conceived a son in her old age, and this is the sixth month for her who was called barren; for nothing will be impossible for God (Luke 1:35-37).

Mary responds with her final response, the gift of her whole self to God to be used however He wishes.

The second means of appreciating who is born, one which is used as the gospel for the Mass during the day, is the prologue of John's Gospel:

> In the beginning was the Word, and the Word was with God, and the Word was God. He was in the beginning with God (John 1:1-2).

These few words contain a world of meaning. "In the beginning" reminds us of the first words of Genesis. Then, "the Word," which recalls Wisdom 7:23-30, is changed to "the Word" because *lógos* is masculine, while *sophía* (wisdom) is feminine. The Word was in dynamic relationship with *the* God (the Father) and the Word was God (Divine). He was in the beginning in dynamic relationship with God:

> All things came to be through him, and without him nothing came to be. What came to be through him was life, and this life was the light of the human race; the light shines in the darkness, and the darkness has not overcome it (John 1:3-5).

Through the Word all things came into being, particularly life. And this life (*zoé* = eternal life) was the light of humans shining in the midst of darkness without being either comprehended or extinguished by the darkness:

A man named John was sent from God. He came for testimony, to testify to the light, so that all might believe through him. He was not the light, but came to testify to the light. The true light, which enlightens everyone, was coming into the world (John 1:6-9).

A clear distinction is made between John the Baptizer and Christ. John the Baptizer came only to testify to the light, the revelation of Christ. Life (*zoé*) and light (*phós*), along with love (*agápē*), are the three themes of this Gospel:

He was in the world, and the world came to be through him, but the world did not know him. He came to what was his own, but his own people did not accept him (John 1:10-11).

The Word, through whom all things were made, was in the world and came among his own things, but his own people did not accept him:

But to those who did accept him he gave power to become children of God, to those who believe in his name, who were born not by natural generation nor by human choice nor by a man's decision but of God (John 1:12-13).

The Word gave authority to those who did accept him to become children by being born, not in any human way, but of God himself:

And the Word became flesh and made his dwelling among us, and we saw his glory, the glory as of the Father's only Son, full of grace and truth (John 1:14).

The Word became human in all our human weakness, except sin, and "pitched his tent" among us so that we were able to see his glory, the glory (*dóxa*) of the Father's only Son, full of love and truth:

John testified to him and cried out, saying, "This was he of whom I said, 'The one who is coming after me ranks ahead of me because he existed before me.' " From his fullness we have all received, grace in place of grace, because while the law was given through Moses, grace and truth came through

> Jesus Christ. No one has ever seen God. The only Son, God, who is at the Father's side, has revealed him (John 1:15-18).

From his fullness, we have all received. But grace as we know it today was largely unknown. Hence, it seems more appropriate to speak of "love upon love." Yes, the Law was given through Moses, but love and truth came through Christ. Not that one has ever seen God, but God's only Son, who is in the Father's bosom, has revealed Him.

Finally, let us look at Paul's masterly description of the incarnation, death, and resurrection of Jesus, all for the sake of teaching humility to the Philippians:

> Have among yourselves the same attitude that is also yours in Christ Jesus, Who, though he was in the form of God, did not regard equality with God something to be grasped (Phil 2:5-6).

Have the humility of Jesus, Who, though he was God, did not consider equality with God something to be grasped or desperately clung to:

> Rather, he emptied himself, taking the form of a slave, coming in human likeness; and found human in appearance, he humbled himself, becoming obedient to death, even death on a cross (Phil 2:7-8).

Far from clinging desperately to his divine glory, Christ emptied himself totally, taking on the nature of a slave (which we are, in comparison with God). He took on himself our human nature, and found human in appearance, he humbled himself becoming obedient even to his worst creatures. All of this resulted in his death on a cross, the most painful and humiliating death known to man:

> Because of this, God greatly exalted him and bestowed on him the name that is above every name, that at the name of Jesus every knee should bend, of those in heaven and on earth and under the earth, and every tongue confess that Jesus Christ is Lord, to the glory of God the Father (Phil 2:9-11).

Because of Jesus' complete humility and obedience, even to the cross, God has greatly exalted him and has given him a name superior to every other name, one which when mentioned, every knee of every one, even in heaven, should bend, and every tongue should confess that Jesus Christ is Lord of all, in the glory of God the Father.

So now we have looked at three of the most revealing pericopes of sacred Scripture, have examined and paraphrased them in order to arrive at a deeper appreciation of the meaning of the incarnation. But still something is missing. What is it? Simply that, as heirs of two thousand years of Christianity, we tend to take its great mysteries for granted and accept them with no special effort or surprise. But if we had been Jews in the first century, would we have accepted Jesus? After centuries of idolatry, having finally accepted—during the Babylonian Captivity—that there is but one God, we would now, at the time of Christ, have lived monotheistic lives for some five hundred years. In fact, so reverent would we have become that we would not even have pronounced God's sacred name, *Yahweh*. Instead, whenever the name occurred, we would have substituted *adonah* (Lord). After all this, we would probably have considered accepting as Messiah and even Son of God this lowly carpenter of the despised village of Nazareth in Galilee of the Gentiles as preposterous. We would rather have stayed with what was tried and true from our glorious heritage. What humble faith, trust, and love those men and women exhibited who accepted him for what he claimed to be and *was*.

Unfortunately, we cannot wipe out the past two thousand years and place ourselves in the position of the first-century Jew. Is there any other way in which we can recapture something similar which will enable us to begin to appreciate what a leap of humility and love it was for God to become human like us? I submit that there is a way, and it lies in our knowing as much as we can about our current space age.

You and I are only tiny specks on this minuscule planet known as earth, which is only twenty-five thousand miles around. Light, traveling at an incredible one hundred eighty-six thousand miles a second can circle our planet seven and a half times in one second! We are some ninety-three million miles from the sun which is only a middling star two-thirds of the way out from the center of our native galaxy, popularly known as the Milky Way. Our galaxy, comprising billions of stars, is a hundred thousand light years in diameter. A light year is the distance light travels in a year. In fact, it has recently been discovered that, counting the dark matter involved, our galaxy is closer to seven hundred light years across its surface. And our galaxy is only one of billions of similar galaxies that compose our universe. Ever since the "big bang" some fifteen to twenty million years ago, this entire universe has been expanding so rapidly that we may never know its real size or whether it will ever turn back upon itself and implode.

In comparison with our God, this universe, vast as it is, is nothing. God brought it into existence, and he can as easily obliterate it. And that God, whose greatness boggles the mind, chose to take upon himself our insignificant human nature. Putting aside the glory of the beatific vision and all infused knowledge, God emptied himself by taking on our lowly human nature, being confined for nine months in his mother Mary's womb, and, when born poor and helpless, lying in a manger, "for there was no room for them in the inn." No wonder Richard Crashaw, the great English Catholic poet of the seventeenth century, would cry out when contemplating the Christ Child at Christmas:

> Welcome, all wonders in one sight,
>   Eternity shut in a span,
> Summer in winter, day in night,
>   Heaven in earth and God in man.
> Great little one, whose all-embracing birth
> Lifts earth to heaven, stoops heaven to earth![2]

But what about the theme of this study, namely the indwelling of Christ in the individual human soul? Certainly there is plenty of biblical evidence supporting the view that Christ dwells with those of his followers who are in the state of grace and welcome his presence. For example,

2. Richard Crashaw, "Hymn of the Nativity," *The Complete Poetry of Richard Crashaw*, ed. George W. Williams (New York, New York University Press, 1972) 83.

Whoever loves me will keep my word, and my Father will love him, and we will come to him and make our dwelling with him (John 14:23).

No one has ever seen God. Yet, if we love one another, God remains in us, and his love is brought to perfection in us (1 John 4:12).

Behold, I stand at the door and knock. If anyone hears my voice and opens the door, [then] I will enter his house and dine with him, and he with me (Rev 3:20).

Yet I live, no longer I, but Christ lives in me; insofar as I now live in the flesh, I live by faith in the Son of God who has loved me and given himself up for me (Gal 2:20).

My eager expectation and hope is that I shall not be put to shame in any way, but that with all boldness, now as always, Christ will be magnified in my body, whether by life or by death. For to me life is Christ, and death is gain (Phil 1:20-21).

It is not that I have already taken hold of it or have already attained perfect maturity, but I continue my pursuit in hope that I may possess it, since I have indeed been taken possession of by Christ Jesus (Phil. 3:12).

For this reason I kneel before the Father, from whom every family in heaven and on earth is named, that he may grant you in accord with the riches of his glory to be strengthened with power through his Spirit in the inner self, and that Christ may dwell in your hearts through faith; that you, rooted and grounded in love, may have strength to comprehend with all the holy ones what is the breadth and length and height and depth, and to know the love of Christ that surpasses knowledge, so that you may be filled with all the fullness of God (Eph 3:14-15).

But now [the mystery] has been manifested to his holy ones, to whom God chose to make known the riches of the glory of this mystery among the Gentiles; it is Christ in you, the hope for glory (Col 1:26-27).

Indeed, there is no lack of biblical references to this indwelling in us. But there is a great deal of difference between biblical references and real-life experience. What we are dealing with here is the desire of the risen Christ to continue his life and ministry in and through us by his taking possession of us, with our consent, so that he can see with our eyes, speak with our tongues, hear with our ears, think with our minds, love with our hearts, work with our hands, and suffer with our bodies.

We can feel his presence within us. Granted that it is difficult to explain, we feel within ourselves in an ineffable way the presence, indwelling, love, and peace of Jesus Christ our blessed Lord. The proof that this is so is that we are content to be with Jesus. We seek no other enjoyment.

We are the soil that receives the seed of the Word of God. At the same time as we are celebrating his birth on our earth, he is being born anew within us. Let us nurture and protect this birth within us! Taking a lesson from the sower and seed in Matthew 13:1-9, 18-23, where they were accustomed to sow and then plow the seed underground, let us not be like the wayside where the seed never even takes root, or like the shallow soil on the rock, where the seed grows up quickly in our enthusiasm but, for lack of soil for roots, quickly dies out. Nor let us be like the soil of the thorny ground which in time chokes out the seed. Let us rather be like the good soil, yielding fruit a hundred, sixty, or thirtyfold.

Within the octave of Christmas, we celebrate the feasts of certain notable saints, for example, St. Stephen and St. John, which gives me the opportunity to say something about the saints. In honoring the saints, we are really honoring Christ himself, for what made them saints was the grace and indwelling of Christ himself. Every one of the saints models some feature of the holiness of Christ. No one models them all, not even Mary; but she comes closest to modeling them all. Not to honor the saints is not to honor Christ.

Holy Family

This is true of the two great feasts held on the Sunday after Christmas and the octave of Christmas respectively—the feast of the Holy Family and that of the Maternity of Mary. Of the liturgy of the former, the conclusion of the "C" cycle of readings is, to my thinking, the most instructive:

He went down with them and came to Nazareth, and was obedient to them; and his mother kept all these things in her heart. And Jesus advanced [in] wisdom and age and favor before God and man (Luke 2:51-52).

Frequently we are asked why Jesus needed to spend all those years at Nazareth before beginning his public ministry. In fact, many apocryphal gospels have been written to tell us what Jesus was doing at Nazareth during that time. Luke's Gospel account gives the very best explanation; because he was thoroughly human, he had to learn and grow and reach the heights of contemplative or mystical perfection so that, at his baptism by John the Baptist, the Father could truly say, "You are my beloved Son; with you I am well pleased" (Mark 1:11). Only if we admit that Jesus became as thoroughly human as it was possible for him to become—sin alone excepted—do these verses and the time spent at Nazareth make any sense.

Maternity of Mary

The feast of the Divine Maternity of Mary offers nothing new in its liturgy, but it never fails to recall to my mind a photograph I took with great difficulty in 1954 of a painting of Our Lady with her Child surrounded by the burning bush of Moses that was on the ceiling of the little Greek Orthodox chapel on top of Mount Sinai. My photograph of it still seems to retain its vivid glow, but I have never seen another with which to compare it. I am reminded of that photograph by the third antiphon of today's feast which refers to the burning bush of Moses as a symbol of Mary's perpetual virginity—the fire burned the bush in Exodus 3:2 but did not overcome it, truly a beautiful image of Mary's motherhood and perpetual virginity.

Epiphany

Finally, the Christmas season closes with the great Feast of the Epiphany or Manifestation of Jesus, whose gospel from Matthew 2:1-12 contains the story of the visit of the Wise Men from the East to honor the Christ Child. This is a very beautiful feast and one ideally suited to this season. Just as in nature the growth of the seed is not at all noticeable until a couple of weeks have passed, so also our personal spiritual growth, so hidden from us, becomes manifest now for the first time. What has happened at Christmas begins to become evident at Epiphany.

But Epiphany is only part of the end of the Christmas cycle. Traditionally, this celebration is manifold, comprising—in addition to the Magi—both the baptism of Christ by John the Baptist, at which time the Father acknowledges His Son and the Holy Spirit makes his presence known, and the Marriage Feast of Cana, where Jesus manifests his identity by changing of water into wine. What these three celebrations have in common is that they are all manifestations about Jesus.

Baptism of Jesus

The Baptism of Jesus, which is celebrated by a special feast closing the Christmas season, is particularly noteworthy. Not only is it the official witness of John the Baptist, representing the Old Testament, that Jesus is the Messiah, but even more important, it is the Father's first witness concerning his Son. Jesus needed that long period of growing up at Nazareth not only to qualify as a thirty-year-old who was therefore responsible and ready for public life. In addition, he was thoroughly human and had to grow "[in] wisdom and age and favor before God and man" (Luke 2:52). Jesus needed that time in order to grow to the heights of mystical experience so that at his baptism by John he would hear those heavenly words from the Father in Mark 1:11, "You are my beloved Son; with you I am well pleased." In his usual blunt way, Mark has the Father address these words directly to Jesus. Likewise, in Mark's Gospel, the Holy Spirit not only comes to rest on Jesus, but actually enters into him, filling him with himself, driving him into the desert to be tempted by the devil, and, in fact, driving him throughout his life and death. In the context of personal spiritual growth, the Holy Spirit will in time also come to drive us through life in order to transform us into Christ.

3 ORDINARY TIME I

Meaning Explained

Now comes a brief but important period in the Church's year and in our personal spiritual growth. It is the first of two periods of Ordinary Time, the time between Epiphany and Ash Wednesday, which will vary in length depending on the date of Easter for the year.

It is called Ordinary Time, but we are cautioned to keep in mind that time is never ordinary because it is the stuff of our eternity. Indeed, our eternity will be happy or miserable or somewhere between, depending on our use of that precious gift of God, time. Let us not lose a second of this great commodity. The Book of Ecclesiastes 3:1-8 has some precious things to say about time:

> There is an appointed time for everything,
> and a time for every affair under the heavens.
> A time to be born, and a time to die;
> a time to plant, and a time to uproot the plant.
> A time to kill, and a time to heal;
> a time to tear down, and a time to build.
> A time to weep, and a time to laugh;
> a time to mourn, and a time to dance.
> A time to scatter stones, and a time to gather them;
> a time to embrace, and a time to be far from embraces.
> A time to seek, and a time to lose;
> a time to keep, and a time to cast away.
> A time to rend, and a time to sew;
> a time to be silent, and a time to speak.
> A time to love, and a time to hate;
> a time of war, and a time of peace.

A little further on, the preacher (Ecclesiastes) has this profound statement to make in Ecclesiastes 3:11:

> He has made everything appropriate to its time, and has put the timeless into their hearts, without men's ever discovering, from beginning to end, the work which God has done.

Viewed in the context of the entire Church year, Ordinary Time is a time of early growth. We left off the Christmas cycle with the feast of the Epiphany (and baptism) of Jesus, where we saw for the first time the beginning of the growth of the Word of God, born in our hearts at Christmas. This now continues in Ordinary Time I.

Candlemas

During this time, a major feast occurs which beautifully brings out this lesson: the feast of the Dedication (Presentation or Consecration) of the Lord, usually called Candlemas Day. On this feast, Mary and Joseph, as devout Jews, dutifully fulfill the directions found in Exodus 13:1-2, 11-15:

> The Lord spoke to Moses and said, "Consecrate to me every first-born that opens the womb among the Israelites, both of man and beast, for it belongs to me. . . .
>
> When the Lord, your God, has brought you into the land of the Canaanites, which he swore to you and your fathers he would give you, you shall dedicate to the Lord every son that opens the womb; and all the male firstlings of your animals shall belong to the Lord. Every first-born of an ass you shall redeem with a sheep. If you do not redeem it, you shall break its neck. Every first-born son you must redeem. If your son should ask you later on, 'What does this mean?' You shall tell him, 'With a strong hand the Lord brought us out of Egypt, that place of slavery. When Pharaoh stubbornly refused to let us go, the Lord killed every first-born in the land of Egypt, every first-born of man and of beast. This is why I sacrifice to the Lord everything of the male sex that opens the womb, and why I redeem every first-born of my sons.' "

Especially noteworthy on the occasion of this feast are the person and prophecies of the ancient Simeon who had been promised that he would not die until he had seen the Messiah. When the Child Jesus was brought in for redemption, Simeon took him in his arms and blessed him, saying,

> Now, Master, you may let your servant go
> in peace, according to your word,
> for my eyes have seen your salvation,
> which you prepared in sight of all the peoples,
> a light of revelation to the Gentiles,
> and glory for your people Israel (Luke 2:29-32).

Then, after a brief interval, he declares further,

> Behold, this child is destined for the fall and rise of many in Israel, and to be a sign that will be contradicted (and you [Mary] yourself a sword will pierce) so that the thoughts of many hearts may be revealed (Luke 2:34).

Undoubtedly this feast has come to include the blessing of candles because Jesus is called "the light for revelation to the Gentiles." And in the context of personal spiritual growth, what we are celebrating is the benefit of Jesus to both Gentiles and Jews and his growth within us. The entire season of Ordinary Time I displays extraordinary growth because it comes between the infancy of Jesus and his maturity. Thirty years of his life are covered in this brief period between the Epiphany (and Baptism) of Jesus and Ash Wednesday, which is the beginning of the Easter cycle. And the Church is as silent about this period of Ordinary Time I as she was about the thirty years at Nazareth.

Why must there be two periods of Ordinary Times? Because they reflect the nature of being, and especially humanity. In the first period of Ordinary Time I, we see the brief and borrowed growth of the Word of God in our individual human nature. In the second one, Ordinary Time II, we will behold our human nature influenced by the saving events at Jerusalem. We will see our human nature transformed into Christ and operating not merely as human but, above all, as divine *and* human.

4 THE EASTER CYCLE

This is the oldest and most meaningful cycle of the Church year. Just as the Church's kerygma or public proclamation about Jesus begins with the saving events in Jerusalem, so too it was logical that the first episodes of Jesus' life that began to be celebrated annually were the passion and resurrection of our Lord. The Church had long since begun to celebrate Sunday as the Christian Sabbath, honoring all Three Persons of the Blessed Trinity. The Father began creation, the Son rose from the dead, and the Holy Spirit descended on the young Church, all on the first day of the week, Sunday. But the Church still wanted to capture the fervor of the saving events annually, and she did so by the end of the second century. That was the beginning of the Church year. Later, the Christmas cycle was added to it, and eventually it evolved into the entire liturgical year as we know it.

But our consideration accepts the Church year as it now stands, without a great deal of historical data and centered around personal spiritual growth. In this as in all other matters regarding the Church year, the Easter triduum and Easter with its octave takes center stage. Everything else is secondary.

The Easter cycle is divided into four parts: the season of Lent; the Triduum; Easter Sunday and its Octave; and the Easter season ending with the Ascension and Pentecost. This is the most fruitful episode in the Church's life. It should also be a precious time of personal spiritual growth. But alas, such is not always the case. It is so much easier, more acccording to our human nature, to contemplate the little Christ Child in the crib at Bethlehem than it is to contemplate Jesus in the midst of his sufferings for us and in his risen state, of which we have no human experience. We have all seen newborn babies and our hearts go out to them. They do not have to do anything to win our love and approval. But when have we ever seen a risen person, and how are we to make the association with such a risen person real in our lives? The answer to that difficult question lies in the realm of the spirit. To repeat St. Paul, if we are content to live the life of the flesh, taking our possessions and pleasures from the world where they are offered very alluringly, then we shall never relate to the risen Christ. In his risen state, particularly, his is a spiritual existence, and only the person who lives the life of the spirit is capable of understanding, loving, and living it fully. In this endeavor, every person who influences our spiritual life is important.

Season of Lent

Just as the Christmas cycle contains the Advent season as a time of preparing by plowing and harrowing the soil, so too the Easter cycle contains an even longer period of preparation, but one of weeding and pruning. Different from Advent which works best on the supposition that nothing has yet been planted and we are plowing and harrowing for our first planting, Lent presumes that the Word of God has been planted at Christmas and has grown since then, but not without weeds and other dependencies. So our main task in Lent is to know ourselves, to weed and prune what has grown within us, and to make our planting as healthy as possible by pruning it so that each branch will bear a good amount of sweet fruit. As I mentioned earlier in this study, the fruit at the end of the Church's year will depend for its quality and quantity on the amount and health of the blossoms produced at Easter time.

Lent is also a remembrance and reliving of the forty days of fasting and enduring of temptations which Jesus underwent immediately after his baptism by John and before his public ministry could formally begin. That is why, on the First Sunday of Lent we are always treated to the temptations of Jesus in the gospels. Matthew and Luke take their story of the temptations from "Q" (*Quelle* = source in German), a theoretical source that contains what is common to Matthew and Luke but not found in Mark. Many theologians think it may have been a dramatization, for who was there? Only Jesus and Satan. Satan was no more inclined to tell of his defeats than was the Pharaoh of Egypt. And it is difficult to picture Jesus, one night while sitting around the apostolic campfire, saying to the apostles, "Did I ever tell you about my temptations?" But it is this dramatized form found in Matthew and Luke that we remember rather than the laconic version in Mark 1:12-13:

> At once the Spirit drove him out into the desert and he remained in the desert for forty days, tempted by Satan. He was among wild beasts, and the angels ministered to him.

It is also this dramatized version that people remember rather than John's Gospel which puts the temptations in far more natural settings—the first in John 6:25-35, the second in John 6:15, and the third in John 7:2-19.

During this time of weeding and pruning, it is important to be in daily touch with both the temptations of Jesus and those very private lesions in our own lives which call out for remedies. Let us see, then, just how the Church aids us by her liturgy.

To assist us in this endeavor, the Church gives us an array of Scripture readings that stimulate our thought processes. Each day, and not just on Sundays, we are presented with matched readings from the Bible. We are invited to read them carefully and then meditate on them or contemplate them, according to our state of soul. It can be helpful to designate one virtue or vice to work on in a given week. The ones which attract me most and are most helpful to me are the five virtues of our Vincentian community: simplicity, humility, meekness, mortification, and zeal for the salvation of the world. During the week, if people seek a way to make each day more effective, they might contemplate one of the seven deadly sins on each day of the week: pride, covetousness, lust, anger, gluttony, envy, and sloth. However, these are only possible aids. The important thing is to use the Scriptures to grow spiritually.

Lent begins with Ash Wednesday when ashes are imposed on us and we are reminded that we are but dust and ashes. Of the Scripture readings for that day, the second one captures the idea of reconciliation that is at the heart of Lent. Let me quote the passage in full from 2 Corinthians 5:20 to 6:2:

> So we are ambassadors for Christ, as if God were appealing through us. We implore you on behalf of Christ, be reconciled to God. For our sake he made him to be sin who did not know sin, so that we might become the righteousness of God in him. Working together, then, we appeal to you not to receive the grace of God in vain. For he says: "In an acceptable time I heard you, and on the day of salvation I helped you." Behold, now is a very acceptable time; behold, now is the day of salvation.

There is something noteworthy about the Scripture readings for the season of Lent. Recall that the readings in Advent all seem to point toward the coming birth of the Savior, Jesus. In Lent, the first three weeks are concerned with our being humble, pure, and loving toward God and others. The second three weeks, those after Laetare Sunday, are quite different. The gospel readings are almost exclusively from John and always contain some element of life; they look toward the resurrection of Jesus, who is "the resurrection and the life" (John 11:25). In our personal spiritual growth, we should follow the Church's lead in this as in all matters. We should not devote the whole of Lent to going over the past but should, with the Church, turn toward "life" in the second half of Lent and prepare ourselves to celebrate Christ, our risen life.

The principal sacrament which we are asked to use to make Lent a holy and freeing season is the Sacrament of Reconciliation, which we will consider briefly. First, note that in 2 Kings 5 in the story of Naaman, the Syrian General with leprosy was not cured until, at the suggestion of his followers, he agreed to the prophet Elisha's command that he wash seven times in the river Jordan. While one could think of all kinds of other and better ways for Naaman to be healed, it was God's way that would actually accomplish it. Secondly, note in John 20:21-22 that it was on the very day of his resurrection from the dead that Jesus actually confers on his apostles the power to forgive sin:

> [Jesus] said to them again, "Peace be with you. As the Father has sent me, so I send you." And when he had said

this, he breathed on them and said to them, "Recieve the holy Spirit. Whose sins you forgive are forgiven them, and whose sins you retain are retained."

Third, note that the most perfect example of reconciliation occurs in Luke 15:11-31. The Greek word for sin is *hamartía* (missing the mark, going astray), and the younger son certainly uses his share of the inheritance to go astray, to estrange himself from his father. The Greek word for repentance is *metánoia* (an about-face, a conversion), and the prodigal son certainly does an about-face when he looks into his heart and sees how wretched he is, then swallows his pride and returns to his father. The Greek word for confession is *homología* (saying the same thing, conceding), and the son does this when he confesses his sin to his father. Finally, the Greek word for reconciliation is *katallagé* (changing, exchanging, restoring to favor), and the father and son end by reconciling with each other and enjoying the fruit of that reconciliation.

However, there is another son involved, and we find it very easy to identify with him and deplore the father's lack of consideration for him. But let us compare this parable of Luke with another Lucan parable, that of the Pharisee and the publican in Luke 18:9-14. We see in the elder son the same kind of attitude that merited condemnation for the Pharisee.

So let the sacrament of reconciliation be prominent during this holy season of Lent, but let it be a program of purification, not just a series of single acts of forgiveness. Let us isolate our principal sins or faults and set out on a carefully planned program of conversion and reconciliation from which we will soon begin to see the results of our endeavors.

Annunciation

In Lent, we are invited to celebrate a most important feast day, the feast of the Annunciation and the Incarnation, which falls on March 25th, exactly nine months before December 25, Jesus' birthday. The Scripture readings for this feast are beautiful, being, in the main, the story of the Emmanuel prophecy in the first reading from Isaiah 7:10-14 and, for the gospel, the actual annunciation account. I have already commented on that in some detail under the heading of Advent. However, I would like to emphasize that this is primarily a feast of our Lord, his actual incarnation, when the "Word became flesh" (John 1:14). When we stop to think about it, what a world-shaking event it was that God should become man. I am reminded of the beautiful Basilica of the Annunciation in the heart of Nazareth. Entering the church, one is immediately struck by the huge opening in the floor of the basilica. When one finds the stairs that lead downward, one eventually comes to the ancient grotto where, on the front of the altar, there is a Jerusalem Cross and, around the cross, the brief inscription so full of meaning: *Verbum caro hic factum est*, which means, "the Word was made flesh here"—the place of the incarnation! The very thought of it sends chills through my body. If the star marking the place of the birth of Christ at Bethlehem is important, equally important or even more so is the site of the incarnation where the Word first took upon himself our human nature in his mother's virgin womb and where he would remain for nine months until his precious birth at Bethlehem.

Even before the annunciation, the Church invites us on March 19th to the Feast of St. Joseph, husband of Mary, protector of the Child Jesus, and patron of the Church. Since this is Lent, however, this March celebration is muted, so an additional feast is added, that of St. Joseph the Worker on May 1st which is the traditional date for workers to celebrate, especially in Communist countries.

Having briefly considered the role of the season of Lent in the Church year, particularly when treated in the context of our personal spiritual growth, let us now examine the main thrust of the Church year, both historically and spiritually—the Easter Triduum.

Having weeded and pruned in fulfillment of the six weeks of Lent, we are now ready to celebrate Easter, the resurrection of our Lord. But before we arrive at the resurrection itself, we must first examine the Easter Triduum—Holy Thursday, Good Friday, and Holy Saturday—and before that, we must celebrate the previous Sunday which is Passion Sunday, popularly called Palm Sunday.

Palm Sunday

On Palm Sunday, we celebrate two things especially—the entry of Jesus as Messiah into Jerusalem and the passion according to Matthew, Mark, or Luke, depending on the cycle. The accounts of the entry into Jerusalem are basically the same, except for the cry of the people which varies according to cycle:

> Cycle 1. "Hosannah to the Son of David;
>> blessed is he who comes in the name of the Lord;
>> hosannah in the highest" (Matt 21:9).
>
> Cycle 2. "Hosannah!
>> Blessed is he who comes in the name of the Lord!
>> Blessed is the kingdom of our father
>>> David that is to come!
>> Hosannah in the highest!" (Mark 11:9-10).
>
> Cycle 3. "Blessed is the king who comes in the name of the Lord.
>> Peace in heaven and glory in the highest"
>> (Luke 19:38).
>
> Cycle 4. "Hosannah!
>> Blessed is he who comes in the name of the Lord,
>> [even] the King of Israel" (John 12:13)."

Regarding the gospels or passions read on this Sunday according to the cycle, each account is written to fit in with the rest of the gospel account. The Gospel of John is reserved for Good Friday.

But the other Scripture readings are extremely appealing: the first reading is the Servant Song from Isaiah 50:4-7; the responsorial psalm is taken from the Messianic twenty-second Psalm; the second reading is the Hymn of Christ from Philippians 2:6-11. After readings of this caliber, anything but the passion account would be anticlimactic.

Triduum

Holy Thursday

There are two distinct celebrations this day, that of the blessing of the Holy Oils and that of the Holy Eucharist, commonly called the *Mandatum* or Maundy Thursday. Each has a role to play in the sanctification of the person, especially if that person is a priest, for it is easy to see that the whole collection of readings is geared to the priests, in union with their bishop. The first reading is from the messianic Isaiah 61 to which Jesus referred in Luke's account of the initial manifestation at Nazareth that he was the Messiah, and indeed that is precisely the gospel reading. The middle reading is a beautiful passage from the Apocalypse or Book of Revelation 1:4-8, which it is worthwhile for us to quote in full:

> Grace to you and peace . . . from Jesus Christ, the faithful witness, the firstborn of the dead and ruler of the kings of the earth. To him who loves us and has freed us from our sins by his blood, who has made us into a kingdom, priests for his God and Father, to him be glory and power forever [and ever]. Amen. Behold, he is coming amid the clouds, and every eye will see him, even those who pierced him. All the peoples of the earth will lament him. Yes. Amen. "I am the Alpha and the Omega," says the Lord God, "the one who is and who was and who is to come, the almighty."

The Mass for the people on the evening of Maundy Thursday is indeed that, with Scripture readings reflecting the Passover regulations from Exodus 12:1-8, 11-14. The responsorial psalm is the beautiful Psalm 116, "How can I repay the Lord for all the good done for me?" The second reading is from 1 Corinthians 11:23-26, the oldest of the four accounts of the institution of the Eucharist. And the gospel is none other than the opening of the Last Supper in John's Gospel 13:1-15, the story of Jesus' washing his disciples' feet and then commanding them to do likewise to one another. The two concepts are closely related. For we can hardly participate in the Eucharist, we can hardly receive the same Body and Blood of Jesus Christ unless we are willing to wash one another's feet. At this particular Mass, the unique things are the washing of the feet after the homily and the transfer of the Holy Eucharist to the altar of veneration after Mass.

But our thoughts on Maundy Thursday go beyond the washing of feet and the transfer of the Eucharist. On this anniversary of its institution, we are filled with gratitude and awe at the humility and love shown us in this gift. Exactly how Christ, working through his priests, changes bread and wine into his own Body and Blood remains a mystery, but that he does so is abundantly clear both from Scripture and from Church history. I have already treated the Bible in regard to the Real Presence earlier in this work, but here let me briefly cover the historical question. Historically, while there was an abundance of heresies regarding the incarnation and the Trinity, there were no heresies or even controversies about the Real Presence of Jesus Christ in the Eucharist until the ninth century when there was such a dispute between St. Paschasius and another monk, Ratramnus, who recanted his position before he died. After that, we did not have another heresy regarding the Eucharist until the eleventh century when Berengarius of Tours flatly denied the Real Presence. Even then, Berengarius likewise recanted before he died. Things remained very much the same from then until the days of John Hus, Philip Wyclif, and Ralph Waldo, but their influence was meager. Basically, it was not until the time of Zwingli that disbelief in the Real Presence became a part of the lore of Protestantism. Yet even then, it was not universal, for Martin Luther never denied it, nor did the original Anglicans. While many today deny or doubt the Real Presence, we who take our Lord's words at face value uphold it with gratitude and awe, and each Holy Thursday gives us the opportunity to reaffirm our faith in it.

But the use of the gospel of the washing of the feet at the Last Supper introduces another note into the celebration, one of sharing and service. There is a natural affinity between the reception of Our Lord in Holy Communion and our sharing with others the gifts that we have received from God.

I am reminded here of that powerful parable which God himself has given us in the very land of Israel. In the north stands the beautiful Sea of Galilee, over six hundred feet below sea level at its highest point and over twelve hundred feet below sea level at its lowest point. Jesus' favorite among all the holy places because of the beauty of its scenery and the abundance of its fish, the Sea of Galilee receives abundant water from the Bekah Valley in what is now Lebanon, and it passes its surplus water on into the river Jordan. The river Jordan, some sixty miles in length as the crow flies but over two hundred miles long as the river winds, then passes its water on into the Dead Sea. But the Dead Sea, over thirteen hundred feet below sea level at its highest point and over twenty-six hundred feet below sea level at its lowest point, is just the opposite of the Sea of Galilee. Not only are there no fish, but one cannot even drown in it, it is so full of salt and other chemicals. Why such a sharp contrast when both seas use the same water? The answer is quite simple. The Dead Sea is so far below sea level that it has no outlet, no exit. The water simply evaporates, leaving behind more and more salt and other chemicals. If we who receive an abundance of God's blessings throughout our lives, especially when receiving Holy Communion, share those blessings with others, then like the Sea of Galilee, we always remain pure and beautiful and rich and alive. However, if, like the Dead Sea, we have no outlet and hoard our blessings to ourselves, then we will find ourselves always dead, lifeless, poor, and spiritually destitute. This Palestinian parable challenges us all with its powerful message.

But it raises a question: How can we share what we have received with others? Jesus himself gives us an answer in the Sermon on the Mount:

> You are the salt of the earth. But if salt loses its taste, with what can it be seasoned? It is no longer good for anything but to be thrown out and trampled underfoot. You are the light of the world. A city set on a mountain cannot be hidden. Nor do they light a lamp and then put it under a bushel basket; it is set on a lampstand, where it gives light to all in the house. Just so, your light must shine before others, that they may see your good deeds and glorify your Heavenly Father (Matt 5:13-16).

In our day of salt substitutes and glorious electricity, natural salt and light are not so essential. But in the first century of our era, both of them were considered indispensable. Salt was so necessary, before refrigeration and the discovery of other spices, that Roman soldiers were paid partly in salt, a *salarium* which translates into today's "salary." Light from the sun was so indispensable that Jesus himself does not hesitate to say in John 9:4-5.

> We have to do the works of the one who sent me while it
> is day. Night is coming when no one can work. While I am
> in the world, I am the light of the world.

Now, careful consideration of the matter reveals that we are
able to share Christ with others in three ways: 1) by witness-
ing to him by the way in which we live; 2) by serving others,
particularly by developing and using our charismatic gifts
which, by definition, are to be used in the service of others
(Eph 4:12); 3) by suffering in union with the sufferings of Christ
for the good of others. After all, Jesus did not save the world
by his activity, his preaching, or his miracles, but by his suffering, death, and resurrection.

Good Friday

Here we have the opportunity to be with Jesus throughout
all his sufferings, to offer our own sufferings in union with
his, and to so live that his sufferings may not have been in
vain, at least where we are concerned. We feel a deep debt
of gratitude to a friend who puts his own life in danger in order
to save us. That is understandable, but should we not feel an
overwhelming sense of gratitude to him who has given his life
that we might live? Perhaps, however, we are thinking that
he saved the whole world, and we as individuals are only insignificant particles. If this is what we think, then we do not know
God! Were I the only person on this earth, I have no doubt
that he would have done the same. As God, he is so great that
he dwarfs the universe, but in that greatness, he loves each
of us personally with a deep and personal love. We are what
we are only because he has loved us and protected us.

Good Friday's ceremonies are unique in the Church's year.
They begin with a silent procession up to the altar where the
celebrant, in red vestments, prostrates himself in imitation of
Jesus' prostration in the Garden of Gethsemane. Then, after
a brief prayer, we have the reading of the Suffering-Servant-
of-Yahweh prophecy from Isaiah 52:13-53:12; then the responsorial, Psalm 31, followed by a reading from the great Epistle
to the Hebrews, 4:14-16; 5:1-9. After these preparations, we
read the passion account from the great Gospel of John.

When the passion of John is finished, we have the general intercession for everyone, both inside and outside the Church. These are the most solemn and useful petitions of the entire year. Besides showing a sense of our total dependence on God for everything, these prayers—offered today when we are commemorating the death of Jesus for us—are efficacious in the extreme.

Now comes the heart of the Good Friday service, the solemn veneration of the cross on which Jesus died for us. This is not meant as a once-a-year reverence of the cross, but should reflect our habitual attitude toward our own cross of pain and suffering in this life. If we receive it but then try to hold it out, away from ourselves, how heavy it is. On the other hand, if we receive it, embrace it, and hold it close to ourselves, how much easier it is to carry.

Finally, we receive Holy Communion from the hosts which were presanctified. This is no Mass since there is no conversion of bread and wine into the sacred Body and Blood of Christ. Because we receive that which was already consecrated, this service is traditionally known as the Mass of the Presanctified.

Whether our Good Friday will be helpful to us in our personal spiritual growth depends entirely on whether we truly enter into the thoughts of the Scripture readings and the symbolism of the actions involved. As we have often indicated, we can inform both by words which have the power to move us and by symbolism which, if we embrace as intended, has the power not only to move us but to transform us into what God wants us to be.

Holy Saturday and the Easter Vigil

At one time in the Church, the Easter vigil service was the principal service of the year. The reason is not hard to find. It stems from a proper understanding of the words and ceremonies of this day. The Easter vigil marks the resurrection of our Lord and Savior, Jesus Christ. Everything about it—the lighting of new fire; lighting of the paschal candle (which represents the risen Christ until Pentecost and at baptism); singing of the *Exultet*; proclaiming of the Scriptures, of which there are at least seven taken from the Old Testament as a kind of brief history of God's mercy and goodness in our salvation; the blessing of the baptismal and other holy water, the baptism of some adults and children; and the offering of the Holy Sacrifice of the Eucharist—is designed, not just to be repeated over and over, not just to make the saving events present to us, but pre-eminently to involve us so that we offer ourselves and partici-pate in all that our holy Church has to offer. To this end, to an understanding of baptism as participation in the death and resurrection of Jesus and hence to an understanding of the resurrection itself, the middle reading for the Easter vigil is al-ways from Paul's letter to the Romans, 6:3-11:

> Or are you unaware that we who were baptized into Christ Jesus were baptized into his death? We were indeed buried with him through baptism into death, so that, just as Christ was raised from the dead by the glory of the Father, we too might live in newness of life.
>
> For if we have grown into union with him through a death like his, we shall also be united with him in the resurrec-tion. We know that our old self was crucified with him, so that our sinful body might be done away with, that we might no longer be in slavery to sin. For a dead person has been absolved from sin. If, then, we have died with Christ, we believe that we shall also live with him. We know that Christ, raised from the dead, dies no more; death no longer has power over him. As to his death, he died to sin once and for all; as to his life, he lives for God. Consequently, you too must think of yourselves as [being] dead to sin and liv-ing for God in Christ Jesus.

Since baptism is one of the main features of this ceremony—as evidenced both by the baptism of adults during the service and by the renewal of baptismal promises made by the entire congregation—it is well that we look at the various elements in this beautiful sacrament which (like circumcision for the Jews) enabled us to become children of the new covenant and of the Christian Church.

Going to the heart of the matter, the pouring of the water accomplishes the washing away of original and all actual sins, but more than that. We must remember that water meant life, particularly in John's Gospel. So in baptism, the pouring of the water signifies the giving of life *(zoé)*, the very life of Christ himself. Christ is born in us through baptism. But that is only the beginning. He desires to grow in us, throughout our lives, by means of our prayer, good deeds, and the reception of the sacraments.

Before and after the pouring of the water, there are two anointings; one on the chest with the oil of catechumens, the other on the forehead with the oil of sacred chrism. The first anointing is optional, but I always like to use it because it recalls for us what St. Paul says: Like contestants in ancient times who anointed their whole bodies for the struggle, throughout our lives we also will be in constant struggle between living the life of the spirit (striving for union with God) and living the life of the flesh (inclined to temptation and sin).

The second anointing is even more important. First of all, chrism was used in the anointing of kings, priests, and prophets; we are being anointed to all three of those great roles. Second, chrism sets us apart from other men and women and indicates that we now belong to God. Belonging to God puts us under obligation to live for him alone. Third, chrism consecrates us to God as holy and pure subjects of worship. Two stories in the Old Testament bring out something of the meaning of this consecration. The first story is that of Samson, in Judges 13-16, who was consecrated from his mother's womb by Nazirite vow. As long as he was faithful to the requirements of that vow—not drinking anything alcoholic and not cutting his hair—he was the superman of his time, doing all manner of deeds requiring superhuman strength. But as soon as he told Delilah the secret of his consecration and his hair was cut, he became like any other man and was captured by the Philistines who gouged out his eyes and put him to grinding grain like an animal. But the Philistines neglected one little detail. They let his hair grow out again, symbolic of his reconsecration, and he was able to pull down the entire temple of Dagon on the Philistine royalty, nobility, and their wives. The power of consecration!

The second story, from the fifth chapter of Daniel, is even more dramatic. Belshazzar, grandson of Nebuchadnezzar, was reigning in Babylon; one evening he decided to throw a huge banquet—actually an orgy—for himself, his courtiers, and their wives and concubines. During the orgy, which was a bad idea, he had another poor idea: to bring in the sacred vessels brought back from the temple in Jerusalem by his grandfather Nebuchadnezzar and desecrate them during the orgy. While they desecrated the sacred vessels, a disembodied hand appeared, writing on the wall opposite him, *Mene, mene, thekel, upharsim.* Belshazzar was frightened to the core. He knew that this was a bad omen, but not what it meant. First, he called in his Babylonian soothsayers, who read the words as nouns, names of coins. They could not make heads or tails of the writing.

Then he called in Daniel and offered him gifts if he could interpret the saying. Daniel refused the gifts, but interpreted the saying, not as nouns but as verbs: *Mene,* God has numbered your kingdom and put an end to it. *Thekel,* you have been weighed in the balance and found wanting. And *Upharsim,* your kingdom has been divided and given to the Medes and Persians. All these things happened that very same night! If this is the punishment for profaning consecrated vessels, what can we say about the profaning of living, consecrated human vessels? St. Paul's words in 1 Corinthians 6:18-20 speak to this point:

> Avoid immorality. Every other sin a person commits is outside the body, but the immoral person sins against his own body. Do you not know that your body is a temple of the holy Spirit within you, whom you have from God, and that you are not your own? For you have been purchased at a price. Therefore glorify God in your body.

Besides the anointing with sacred chrism, the sacrament of baptism contains two more symbols which have a deep meaning for us. The first one is the placing of the white garment on the newly baptized. This reminds us that we are to lead a pure life, but there is a still deeper symbolism involved. In two places in Scripture, Paul reminds us that we are called upon to ''put on'' the Lord Jesus, that is, to clothe ourselves in Christ much as an actor puts on the mask and costume of the person whose role he is playing. In Galatians 3:27, Paul says: ''For all of you who were baptized into Christ have clothed yourselves with Christ.'' And in Romans 13:14, he says: "But put on the Lord Jesus Christ, and make no provision for the desires of the flesh."

The second symbol is the giving of the lighted candle to the child's father with appropriate words. This recalls that Jesus said, "You are the light of the world" (Matt 5:14). But we are reminded, in John 8:12 and 9:5, that Jesus proclaims that he is the Light of the world. Is there a contradiction here? Not at all. The light of our physical world is the sun, source of our illumination, heat, and even our energy. Christ is certainly like that light to us. We only reflect or, better still, radiate his light to others as Paul points out to us in 2 Corinthians 4:6:

> For God who said, "Let light shine out of darkness," has shone in our hearts to bring to light the knowledge of the glory of God on the face of [Jesus] Christ.

This is a tremendous symbol for our personal spiritual growth, but it will be fulfilled only to the extent that we live out that other statement of St. Paul in 2 Corinthians 3:18:

> All of us, gazing with unveiled face on the glory of the Lord, are being transformed into the same image from glory to glory, as from the Lord who is the Spirit.

Having completed our consideration of Palm Sunday and of Holy Thursday, Good Friday, and the Easter vigil or Holy Saturday Mass, we are now ready to probe the depths of the meaning of Easter from an examination of the Scripture readings for Easter itself and for the entire octave of this greatest of all feasts.

Easter Sunday and Its Octave

I picture Easter Sunday, above all, as a time of flowers, a riot of blooms, a blaze of blossoms. Why? For one thing, it is spring, the feast being celebrated on the first Sunday after the first full moon after the vernal equinox. And spring is a time for flowers. Oh, the other symbols of Easter are generally meaningful—the egg, the rabbit, the butterfly, all carrying with them a modicum of meaning. This is especially true of the butterfly, which passes from the lowly life of a caterpillar to the grand freedom and beauty of a butterfly. If God is capable of forming in one of his humble creatures two such different stages of life, is he not capable of doing something similar for his highest creation?

A few years ago, anxious to honor Easter about which so few songs have been written, I was inspired to write about the beauty of Easter, spring's blooming, and the abundance of flowers that should characterize this feast:

Nature's Easter Parade

Verse: There's a great parade ev'ry Easter morn,
Down New York's famous old Fifth Avenue,
But nothing can compare
With Nature fresh and fair,
Parading all her beauty born anew!

Chorus: It's Easter morning and with the dawning
Comes Nature's great Easter parade,
Dressed up in her lilacs blooming,
Freshened with their sweet perfuming.
The Son is risen and Nature's given
Her reason to promenade,
Topped off with her bright blue bonnet,
Cherry blossoms pink upon it.

Hear the birds sing out their joyous adoration;
Add the words of grateful praise for our salvation.
It's Nature's Birthday, the whole wide
earth's day.
With lilies for candles galore!
Time to join the celebration,
One in tune with all creation!
Praise the Lord we all adore!
Praise the Lord we all adore!

What can justify such extraordinary praise of the resurrection of Christ? Simply this, that by the very fact of it's happening, it provides the whole foundation for our faith, our hope, our love. It is the foundation of our faith because without the resurrection, Jesus is just a dead martyr, lying on a tree; with it, he has overcome death itself and given us assurance of the truth of his words. The resurrection is the foundation of our hope since, without the resurrection, we are prey to all the ills of this world; with it, however, he is and also makes us to be beyond all of our besetting problems. It is the foundation of our love and our life *(agápē* and *zoē)* because without it, we are only creatures of this life which ends with our death; with it, his life continues, both in itself and in us and the end of all our pains and sorrows is eternal life in Christ.

But how are we, twenty centuries after Jesus Christ, going to enter into his resurrection? That is where the liturgy comes in; remember that it is precisely the liturgy which makes present for us the saving events of the life of Christ. By our prayer-life, by the use of the sacraments which he has given to his Church, and above all by the Holy Eucharist, Jesus is as present to us now as he was to Mary and his beloved apostles. That is the beauty of the liturgy. It gives each one of us an opportunity to die and rise with Christ as Paul clearly tells us in Colossians 3:1-4:

> If then you were raised with Christ, seek what is above, where Christ is seated at the right hand of God. Think of what is above, not of what is on earth. For you have died, and your life is hidden with Christ in God. When Christ your life appears, then you too will appear with him in glory.

That is the second reading of today's Mass. The first reading is taken from Acts 10:34, 37-45, in which Peter is trying to make known to Cornelius and his household at Caesarea all that he and the other apostles had witnessed about Jesus, including the resurrection about which Cornelius was anxious to hear. The responsorial psalm is Psalm 118, one which will be repeated often during this holy time, especially verse twenty-four, which becomes a kind of general refrain: ''This is the day the Lord has made; let us rejoice in it and be glad.'' The gospel is John 20:1-9, the story of Peter and John running to the tomb and finding it empty as Mary Magdalene had told them. It is as if the Church wants each one of us to experience the gradual enlightenment of the apostles that led to their belief in the resurrection.

But Easter is more than a particular day; it is a whole octave. And the Scripture readings for the Easter octave are intended to help us to grow in appreciation of Jesus' resurrection and to live the resurrection more fully in our personal lives.

Without going into the matter too fully, let us look now at the Scripture readings for the octave of Easter in order to see there what Christ and the Church have chosen for our personal spiritual growth.

On Easter Monday, the first reading contains Peter's Pentecostal discourse, while the gospel reading is that part of Matthew's Gospel—28:8-15—containing Jesus' appearance to the women, their subsequent silence, and the explanation of how the guards were paid to say that Jesus' disciples had stolen his body while the guards were asleep. As St. Augustine has astutely pointed out, if they were asleep, how did the guards know that it was the disciples of Jesus who had stolen the body?[1]

On Easter Tuesday, for the first reading, the story of Peter on Pentecost continues, the outcome of which is the baptism of some three thousand converts. The gospel continues the account of Mary Magdalene from John's Gospel. After informing Peter and John, as recounted in Sunday's gospel, Mary Magdalene returned to the tomb, seeking some sign of Jesus. Encountering Jesus there but convinced he was the gardener, she begs him for information. Jesus simply says, "Mary!" to which she replies "*Rabbouni!*", for she recognized him and immediately grasped him around the legs. In John 20:17, Jesus responds:

> Stop holding on to me, for I have not yet ascended to the Father. But go to my brothers and tell them, "I am going to my Father and your Father, to my God and your God."

How full of meaning this statement of Jesus is, not only to Mary Magdalene, but to all of us. The expression "Stop holding on to me" or "Do not cling to me" reminds us not to cling to heavenly consolations when Jesus wants to remove them so that we may truly find that his Father is truly our Father and

---

1. This quote is from St. Augustine's comment on Gen 2:28 in "De Genesin ad Litteram." Jacques Paul Migne, *Patres Latini* (1841) 34:278 cited in Pius XII's "Divino Afflante Spiritu," *Rome and the Study of Scripture*, 6th ed. (St. Meinrad, Ind.: Grail Publications, 1958) 82.

his God is truly our God. Such is the power of the resurrection that it has made us Jesus' brothers and sisters. What an ally we have in sacred Scripture, which tells us who and what we are in 1 John 3:1-3:

> See what love the Father has bestowed on us that we may be called the children of God. Yet so we are. The reason the world does not know us is that it did not know him. Beloved, we are God's children now; what we shall be has not yet been revealed. We do know that when it is revealed we shall be like him, for we shall see him as he is. Everyone who has this hope based on him makes himself pure, as he is pure.

Wednesday's Scripture readings feature two pairs of people: Peter and John at the temple's Beautiful Gate in the first reading, and, in the gospel, the two disciples of Emmaus. Most of us instinctively identify with Peter when he responds to the beggar in Acts 3:1-10:

> I have neither silver nor gold, but what I do have I give you: In the name of Jesus Christ the Nazorean, [rise and] walk!

The man rose and walked. In fact, he "went into the temple with them, walking and jumping and praising God." When the people realized that this was the beggar who used to be at the gate called "Beautiful," "they were filled with amazement and astonishment at what had happened to him." But we shall have to wait until tomorrow, Easter Thursday, to learn the aftermath of this episode.

Meanwhile, in Luke 24:13-35, we are treated to the story of the two disciples on their way to Emmaus. In Luke's incomparable style, we see that they are puzzled over the death and then the empty tomb of Jesus. What were they to make of all this? Then Jesus joins them and although the two do not recognize him, in a kind of Liturgy of the Word, he chides them:

> "Oh, how foolish you are! How slow of heart to believe all that the prophets spoke! Was it not necessary that the Messiah should suffer these things and enter into his glory?" Then beginning with Moses and all the prophets, he interpreted to them what referred to him in all the Scriptures.

They were astonished at his knowledge of the Scriptures and, as it was almost evening, they prevailed on him to stay with them. In a kind of Liturgy of the Eucharist,

> It happened that, while he was with them at table, he took bread, said the blessing, broke it, and gave it to them. With that their eyes were opened and they recognized him, but he vanished from their sight.

Excitedly, the two expressed their recognition of him and their amazement:

> Were not our hearts burning [within us] while he spoke to us on the way and opened the Scriptures to us?

So, even though it was night (and people did not usually travel at night for fear of robbers), they returned to Jerusalem where they found the Eleven, who declared, ''The Lord has truly been raised and has appeared to Simon!'' Then the two recounted what had taken place on the way and how he was made known to them in the breaking of the bread.

On Thursday of the octave of Easter, we have a continuation of the account of the cure of the lame man at the Gate called Beautiful (Acts 3:11-26) in which Peter, at the portico of Solomon, addresses the people gathered around the former lame man, telling them that it was Jesus of Nazareth, unjustly condemned by them, who had wrought this miracle. In fact, he says,

> You denied the Holy and Righteous one and asked that a murderer be released to you. The author of life you put to death, but God raised him from the dead; of this we are witnesses.

Then Peter assured them he knew that both they and their leaders had acted in ignorance. Now was their opportunity to repent that their sins might be removed, and after quoting Moses in Deuteronomy 18:15-19, he declares to them:

> You are the children of the prophets and of the covenant that God made with your ancestors when he said to Abraham, ''In your offspring all the families of the earth shall be

blessed.'' For you first, God raised up his servant and sent him to bless you by turning each of you from your evil ways.

The responsorial psalm today is the beautiful Psalm 8:

> O Lord, our Lord,
> How awesome is your name over all the earth!
> What are humans that you are mindful of them,
> mere mortals that you care for them?
> Yet you have made them little less than a god,
> crowned him with glory and honor.
> You have given them rule over the works of your hands,
> Put all things at their feet.
>
> All sheep and oxen,
> even the beasts of the field,
> The birds of the air, the fish of the sea,
> And whatever swims the paths of the seas.

The gospel is also a continuation of the story of the two disciples of Emmaus who have returned to Jerusalem to report their experience of the risen Lord. While they were still speaking, Jesus himself appeared to them, showed them his wounded hands and feet, asked if they had anything to eat, and ate a piece of grilled fish before them. Then he said to them in Luke 24:36-49:

> ''These are my words that I spoke to you while I was still with you, that everything written about me in the law of Moses and in the prophets and psalms must be fulfilled.'' Then he opened their minds to understand the scriptures. And he said to them, ''Thus it is written that the Messiah would suffer and rise from the dead on the third day and that repentance, for the forgiveness of sins, would be preached in his name to all the nations, beginning from Jerusalem. You are witnesses of these things. And [behold] I am sending the promise of my Father upon you; but stay in the city until you are clothed with power from on high.''

According to the Gospel of Luke, those were Jesus' final words.

For Friday of the octave of Easter, the first reading continues the story of the lame beggar, now completely healed. In Acts 4:1-12, the priests arrest Peter and John for preaching about the resurrection; then, the next day, a meeting of the Sanhedrin is held in which Peter and John are challenged to say by what power and name they had done what they did. Peter, filled with the Holy Spirit, speaks up:

> Leaders of the people and elders: If we are being examined today about a good deed done to a cripple, namely, by what means he was saved, then all of you and all the people of Israel should know that it was in the name of Jesus Christ the Nazorean whom you crucified, whom God raised from the dead; in his name this man stands before you healed. He is "the stone rejected by you, the builders, which has become the cornerstone." There is no salvation through anyone else, nor is there any other name under heaven given to the human race by which we are to be saved.

Naturally, the responsorial psalm is Psalm 118, about the stone rejected by the builders that has become the cornerstone or keystone.

The gospel reading is from the first part of the miraculous catch of fish at the Sea of Galilee in John 21:1-14. Seven of the disciples were at the Sea of Galilee; when Peter says, "I am going fishing," they all accompany him. Although they fished all night, they caught nothing. At dawn, a man appeared on the shore who directed them to cast their net to the starboard side; when they did so, they caught one hundred fifty-three large fish. Then they recognized the Master, but no one asked, "Who are you?" The story ends with Jesus' offering his disciples a breakfast of bread and fish, and John's remark that this is the third time Jesus has revealed himself to his disciples since the resurrection.

This may be the same story told in the fifth chapter of Luke's Gospel leading to Jesus' call to the disciples to follow him, since from henceforth, they would catch men. No matter! What is important is the amount of material for our personal spiritual growth.

The Saturday first reading is a continuation of the confrontation of Peter and John with the religious authorities, who feared the people in whose midst the two had worked an obvious miracle. Consequently, in Acts 4:13-21, the leaders ended by simply forbidding them to preach in the name of Jesus

Christ the Nazorean. Peter and John simply but courageously answer:

> Whether it is right in the sight of God for us to obey you rather than God, you be the judges. It is impossible for us not to speak about what we have seen and heard.

The gospel reading, rather than finishing the twenty-first chapter of John concerning the conferral of the primacy on Peter, contains instead the longer ending from the Gospel of Mark (16:9-15). But it is a good summary of the risen Christ's appearances found in the other gospels and closes with Jesus making this incredible statement, ''Go into the whole world and proclaim the gospel to every creature.'' The gospel ends here, but we cannot turn away without finishing the quotation:

> Whoever believes and is baptized will be saved; whoever does not believe will be condemned. These signs will accompany those who believe; in my name they will drive out demons, they will speak new languages. They will pick up serpents [with their hands] and if they drink any deadly thing, it will not harm them. They will lay hands on the sick, and they will recover.

The octave of Easter is the following Sunday, often called Low Sunday—in contrast with Easter—or White Sunday, in reference to the ancient practice of new converts wearing their baptismal robes until the end of the first Sunday after Easter. This was, in a certain sense, their day. The Scripture readings vary, but there is a certain sameness among them. So I will quote or refer to them as first reading, responsorial psalm, second reading, and the gospel.

In the ''A'' cycle, the first reading is one of the descriptions of the early Church in Acts 2:42-47, of which the principal parts are as follows:

> They devoted themselves to the teachings of the apostles and to the communal life, to the breaking of the bread and to the prayers. . . . All who believed were together and had all things in common. . . . Every day they devoted themselves to meeting together in the temple area and to breaking bread in their homes. . . .

Note that the expression, "breaking bread," seems to be Luke's technical phrase for celebrating the Eucharist. Luke provides us with four descriptions of the Church in her infancy, probably in order to keep her ever close to her pristine fervor.

The responsorial psalm is again the 118th Psalm, with emphasis on the love of the Lord as evidenced in the versicle, "Give thanks to the Lord, who is good, whose love endures forever."

The second reading is taken from the First Letter of St. Peter which is, appropriately enough, one or more baptismal homilies. So, in today's section from 1 Peter 1:3-9, we read in part:

> Blessed be the God and Father of our Lord Jesus Christ, who in his great mercy gave us a new birth to a living hope through the resurrection of Jesus Christ from the dead, to an inheritance that is imperishable, undefiled, and unfading, kept in heaven for you who, by the power of God are safeguarded through faith, to a salvation that is ready to be revealed in the final time.
>
> In this you rejoice, although now for a little while you may have to suffer through various trials, so that the genuineness of your faith, more precious than gold that is perishable even though tested by fire, may prove to be for praise, glory, and honor at the revelation of Jesus Christ.
>
> Although you have not seen him you love him; even though you do not see him now yet believe in him, you rejoice with an indescribable and glorious joy, as you attain the goal of [your] faith, the salvation of your souls.

Here, in Peter's first epistle, the language is enough to boggle the mind. How on earth could St. Peter, relatively uneducated and known more for his heart than his head, be capable of writing such a general epistle. The explanation is given in the conclusion of 1 Peter 5:12: "I write you this briefly through Silvanus, whom I consider a faithful brother, exhorting you and testifying that this is the true grace of God." It was during Silvanus' time that Peter managed to write this first epistle.

The gospel reading in the "A" cycle of the Octave of Easter is taken from John 20:19-31 and features several important points: (1) Jesus appears to ten of his apostles, breathes on them, and confers on them the power to forgive sins. (2)

Thomas was absent when Jesus appeared and even though the other apostles faithfully recounted all that Jesus had said and done, he steadfastly refused to believe. (3) Jesus appeared again a week later when Thomas was with the others and invited him to view the marks of the nails in his hands and put his hand into his side, (4) Thomas, completely overcome, exclaims, "My Lord and my God!" (5) Jesus says, "Have you come to believe because you have seen me? Blessed are those who have not seen and have believed!" (6) The Johannine conclusion to his gospel follows where John admits that many things are not included in this book, but that (7) these *are* included so that readers may conclude that Jesus is the Messiah, the Son of God, and that believing this, they "may have life in his name."

I have already discussed forgiveness of sins in the Lenten part of this work and need not repeat it. But I would like to comment briefly about Thomas. John was probably writing his gospel (with the help of his disciples, Polycarp and Prochorus) while Domition, the younger brother of Titus, was emperor. While Titus and his father, Vespasian, were good Emperors, Domition was so much like Nero that he was known widely as *Nero Redivivus*—that is, Nero Reborn. What is even more to the point, he insisted not only on worldwide emperor worship, but his favorite expression, when he was worshipped as emperor, was "My Lord and my God." Thus, this expression of Thomas takes on added meaning not only in the worship of Christ but also in acknowledgement of what Christ has proven to be by his resurrection: he and not Domition has been shown to be the true "Lord and God" of Thomas.

The conclusion to the entire episode is one which John himself attaches to his work. A careful study of the twenty-first chapter reveals that it was not written by John but by one of his disciples, at least in part to show that Jesus never said that John would be around for his second coming but only that it was none of Peter's business what Jesus had in store for John.

The first reading in the "B" cycle, like that of "A", contains another of the acknowledged summaries of early Church life, this one found in Acts 4:32-35:

> The community of believers was of one heart and mind, and no one claimed that any of his possessions was his own, but

they had everything in common. With great power the apostles bore witness to the resurrection of the Lord Jesus, and great favor was accorded them all.

The second part tells how whoever had property would sell it, and give the money to the Church to be used for those in need. In addition to teaching voluntary community of goods, it was preparing the way for what followed: the generosity of Barnabas and the deceit of Ananias and Sapphira who perished because they said they were giving the total amount realized from the sale of their property when in reality they were not.

The responsorial psalm is again Psalm 118 with the refrain, "Give thanks to the Lord, who is good, whose love endures forever."

The second reading is a beautiful one from 1 John 5:1-6:

Everyone who believes that Jesus is the Christ is begotten by God, and everyone who loves the father loves [also] the one begotten by him. In this way we know that we love the children of God when we love God and obey his commandments. For the love of God is this, that we keep his commandments. And his commandments are not burdensome, for whoever is begotten by God conquers the world. And the victory that conquers the world is our faith. Who [indeed] is the victor over the world but the one who believes that Jesus is the Son of God? This is the one who came through water and blood, Jesus Christ, not by water alone, but by water and blood. The Spirit is the one that testifies, and the Spirit is truth.

Probably all of this pericope is clear to the reader, except perhaps the reference to "water and blood." To what does this refer? Most probably to the episode in John 19:34: "But one soldier thrust his lance into his side, and immediately blood and water flowed out." Apparently John sees in this event the birth of the Church and of the whole sacramental system.

The gospel reading for the "B" cycle is still the story of Thomas which we have already considered in the first reading.

In the "C" cycle, the first reading, following the lead of the other two cycles, is another summary of the early church found in Acts 5:12-16:

Many signs and wonders were done among the people at the hands of the apostles. They were all together in Solomon's portico. None of the others dared to join them, but the people esteemed them. Yet more than ever, believers in the Lord, great numbers of men and women, were added to them. Thus they even carried the sick out into the streets and laid them on cots and mats so that when Peter came by, at least his shadow might fall on one or another of them. A large number of people from the towns in the vicinity of Jerusalem also gathered, bringing the sick and those disturbed by unclean spirits, and they were all cured.

This episode of the early Church contains an extraordinary account, the cleansing of the afflicted just by Peter's shadow. Such a thing is not told, even once, about Jesus himself. Is Peter, then, performing even greater things than the Lord? The explanation is quite simple. It is not Peter performing these miracles, but Jesus himself. And this is the meaning of that extraordinary statement at the Last Supper in John 14:12:

> Amen, amen I say to you, whoever believes in me will do the works that I do, and will do greater ones than these, because I am going to the Father.

The explanation is that Christ continues to operate in the Church and especially in his saints, and it is particularly through them that we are to come to him. Again, the responsorial psalm is Psalm 118 with exactly the same versicle as in the other two cycles.

The second reading is borrowed in scattered form from the Book of Revelation; Revelation 1:9-11a, 12-13-17-19 is too beautiful for us to avoid quoting it in full:

> I, John, your brother, who share with you the distress, the kingdom, and the endurance we have in Jesus, found myself on the island called Patmos because I proclaimed God's Word and gave testimony to Jesus. I was caught up in spirit on the Lord's day and heard behind me a voice as loud as a trumpet, which said, "Write on a scroll what you see. . . ." Then I turned to see whose voice it was that spoke to me, and when I turned, I saw seven golden lampstands and in the midst of the lampstands one like a son of man,

> wearing an ankle-length robe, with a gold sash around his chest. . . .
>
> When I caught sight of him, I fell down at his feet as though dead. He touched me with his right hand and said, "Do not be afraid. I am the first and the last, the one who lives. Once I was dead, but now I am alive forever and ever. I hold the keys to death and the netherworld. Write down, therefore, what you have seen, and what is happening, and what will happen afterwards."

There is so much to comment on in this section that I will only be able to touch the highlights. First, the author identifies himself as John. Most Scripture scholars today doubt that the Gospel of John, the three epistles, and the Apocalypse or Book of Revelation were written by the same person. I do not. While it is true that the language and vocabulary of these works ascribed to John are quite different, there are a number of nuances found only in these works. I think John wrote his gospel and at least First John with the help of his disciples, Polycarp and Prochorus, but he was alone on the island of Patmos when he wrote the Book of Revelation.

Next, he identifies himself as sharing in the persecution and as exiled to the island of Patmos for his preaching. He then mentions that he was "caught up in the spirit on the Lord's Day" and heard behind him a voice "like a trumpet" telling him to write to the seven churches of Asia. And when he turned to see the speaker, he received the great vision of Christ surrounded by the seven golden lampstands, a vision similar to Jesus' parable of the true vine and the branches in John 15 or to Paul's parable of the Church as the Body of Christ in 1 Corinthians 12.

When John caught sight of Jesus, who holds the keys to death and the underworld, he fell at his feet as though dead, whereupon Jesus touched him with his right hand and said not to be afraid, that he had been dead but now was alive. Hence, he wanted John to write down what he had seen, what was happening currently, and what was still to be in the future.

The Book of Revelation is probably the most misunderstood book in the Bible. But it should not be. It is probably so frequently misunderstood because it is used as a book of prophecy. Now, there is prophecy in it, especially regarding the *eschaton* or end time in the final chapters; but basically it belongs to a different literary genre, one called apocalyptic. Apocalyptic literature is underground or resistance literature written in a time of persecution to encourage the persecuted without tipping off the persecutors. Hence all the symbolism which is taken, almost in its entirety, from the Old Testament and the New Testament. While the apocalyptic book of the Old Testament is the Book of Daniel, during the intertestamental period there was a veritable flood of apocalyptic writing among the Jews.

The gospel reading continues to be the story of Thomas, as it is in the other two cycles. It is as if the Church wanted to make sure that we all heard the same gospel and responsorial psalm on this day while she did give us some variety in the first and second readings.

Having completed our consideration of Easter day and its octave, and having seen there the richness of God's compassion for us, we are now prepared to examine the Easter season to find there all that Jesus and the Church, through their sacred liturgy, have placed there for our study.

Easter Season

The Easter season, like the season of Lent, contains six Sundays—the traditional forty days—until Pentecost, the final feast. However, unlike Lent, there is more continuity in the daily readings and hence greater help in our personal spiritual growth.

To derive the fruit intended by the Church, it is imperative that we make a clear distinction between the Sunday readings and the daily readings. These latter, which we will consider first, are based entirely on the Acts of the Apostles for the first reading and the Gospel of John for the second. In the process, the whole of Acts is covered, at least beginning from 4:23 which is where we left off in the daily octave readings. The whole of John is also covered, at least beginning with the discourse with Nicodemus in chapter three.

Because Acts and John are read during the daily readings in the easter season and because the readings take each episode in the order of its appearance, I see no reason to follow them carefully to try to explain each episode. Such a commentary would take us far beyond our projected goal. However, I believe it would serve a good purpose to make some comments on the books themselves—the Acts of the Apostles and the Gospel of John—so that we may be more appreciative of each episode when we encounter it.

First, the Acts of the Apostles is really the Acts of Peter and Paul and tells the story of the early Christian Church. What the Book of Numbers was to the Book of Exodus—that is, the history of the early Israelite origins as a people—so the Acts of the Apostles is to the Gospels, notably the Gospel of Luke: the first acts of the community founded by Jesus after his death and resurrection.

The very first verse of Acts, when it is properly translated, provides the reader with the whole idea itself. Unfortunately, neither the New American Bible (even in its revision) nor the Jerusalem Bible captures the proper translation. For that we need to appeal to the Vulgate of St. Jerome, the Douay-Rheims translation, or the Protestant versions. It is simply a question of translating the verb *érxato* (from *árchomai* = I begin). The New American Bible, revised translation, now reads, "In the first book, Theophilus, I dealt with all that Jesus did and taught until the day he was taken up. . . ." That sounds fine until we look at the Greek and realize that an entire Greek verb failed to have been translated. What the sentence should say is, "In the first book, Theophilus, I dealt with all that Jesus *began* to do and to teach until the day he was taken up. . . ." Jesus only *began* in his lifetime. Now that he has died and risen again, he continues to do things and to teach, but now through the Church, now through individuals such as Peter and Paul. A little meditation on this different tranalation will convince the reader that the one word *érxato* makes all the difference in the world.

In any case, it is important to notice that, in Acts, Jesus' life and ministry are largely externalized in the body, which is the Church. I am certainly not negating the internal element, particularly in view of the explanation that has just been given about the proper translation. However, it remains true that Acts is the story of the miraculous development of the Church, which is a corporate whole.

In contrast, the gospel readings taken from John, in one way or another, are all concerned with the personal and mystical growth of God's people. It is a matter of emphasis only. John's Gospel is the story of God's people also, but in a more spiritual, mystical sense. This is brought out notably in the meaning attached to the parable of Jesus in John 15 about the true vine and the branches. Of course the parable concerns the whole Church, but its emphasis is on the hidden, mystical collusion between Jesus and the individual member.

With this explanation of the Acts of the Apostles and the Gospel of John, I believe that the understanding of the Scripture readings in the daily Masses during the Easter season will be much enhanced. Now, let us look at the Sunday readings.

It is difficult to determine exactly how the particular readings for the season of Easter were decided upon. But, as might be expected, there is a definite preference for readings from John for the gospel. Readings taken from Acts match those of the gospel, and the middle reading is chosen to fit the other two. Here is where it varies from Ordinary Time, in which the middle reading is simply in continuation and is not necessarily connected with the other readings.

For the Third Sunday after Easter, the gospel reading is chosen from the story of the two disciples of Emmaus. We have already commented on this. In the "B" cycle, we have the continuation of the Emmaus story, including the appearance of Jesus to the whole group and his eating with them at Jerusalem. For the "C" cycle, we have the appearance of Jesus to the seven disciples at the Sea of Galilee, which has also been sufficiently explained.

The first reading is taken from Acts, Peter's pentecostal discourse; Peter's discourse after the cure of the beggar at the Temple at the Gate called Beautiful is used for the "B" cycle. For the "C" cycle, Peter and John defying the orders of the high priests is chosen. We have already commented on all three of these readings from Acts. That leaves the second reading to provide us with something on which to comment. The second reading in the "A" cycle, from 1 Peter 1:17-21, certainly does:

> Now if you invoke as Father him who judges impartially according to each one's works, conduct yourselves with rever-

ence during the time of your sojourning, realizing that you were ransomed from your futile conduct, handed on by your ancestors, not with perishable things like silver or gold but with the precious blood of Christ as of a spotless unblemished lamb. He was known before the foundation of the world but revealed in the final time for you, who through him believe in God who raised him from the dead and gave him glory, so that your faith and hope are in God.

In the ''B'' cycle, the second reading is from 1 John 2:1-5a:

My children, I am writing this to you so that you may not commit sin. But if anyone does sin, we have an Advocate with the Father, Jesus Christ the righteous one. He is expiation for our sins, and not for our sins only but for those of the whole world. The way we can be sure that we know him is to keep his commandments. Whoever says, ''I know him,'' but does not keep his commandments is a liar, and the truth is not in him. But whoever keeps his word, the love of God is truly perfected in him.

The second reading for the ''C'' cycle, is from John's Revelation 5:11-14:

I looked again and heard the voices of many angels who surrounded the throne and the living creatures and the elders. They were countless in number, and they cried out in a loud voice: ''Worthy is the Lamb that was slain to receive power and riches, wisdom and strength, honor and glory and blessing.''

Then I heard every creature in heaven and on earth and under the earth and in the sea, everything in the universe, cry out: ''To the one who sits on the throne and to the Lamb, be blessing and honor, glory and might, forever and ever.'' The four living creatures answered, ''Amen,'' and the elders fell down and worshiped.

I have quoted those three important intermediate readings from the Third Sunday after Easter (the first after the Easter octave) for a definite purpose: to show how much they carry the theme of the Church. Now, I would invite the reader to scan the rest of the readings from the Easter season and see there the following facts: (1) that after the Third Sunday of Easter until the Ascension, each first reading is from the Acts of the Apostles and each gospel reading is from John, (2) that close inspection of these readings reveals that they are, in both instances, in ascending order, (3) that the intermediate readings also follow a definite order, each in the "A" cycle being from the First Epistle of Peter, each in the "B" cycle being from the First Letter of John, and each in the "C" cycle being from the Book of Revelation, (4) that further close inspection of these readings manifests the fact that they, too, like the first readings and gospel readings, are always quoted in ascending order. Quite remarkable, would you not agree?

Now, let us examine the readings from the Fourth Sunday of Easter because it seems that the Church is trying to stress a particular theme, namely *Jesus the Good Shepherd*. First of all, the gospel readings are all taken from the tenth chapter of John and all, in one way or another, treat Jesus as the Good Shepherd. A quick glance at the other readings reveals that, implicitly and sometimes explicitly, they also treat of Jesus as the Good Shepherd and his followers as his sheep. For the Jews of Jesus' time, this was not merely a pious thought but touched the very basis of the covenant relationship between Yahweh and Israel.

To examine this idea further, let us look back at Sacred Scripture. There, in Genesis 4:2, we find Abel depicted as a shepherd while Cain is a farmer. Next, in Genesis 13:5-6, both Abram and Lot are depicted as shepherds, although some Scripture experts think that they may have been donkey caravaneers between Canaan and Egypt. Moses, in Exodus 3:1-2, was shepherding his father-in-law's flock of sheep when he beheld the bush burning but not being consumed and was chosen to shepherd the flock of God out of Egypt. Finally, David, in 1 Samuel 16:11, was tending his father's flock of sheep when he was anointed by Samuel to shepherd the people of God instead of Saul.

Attributed to David and everybody's favorite, the famous Psalm 23 begins: "The Lord is my shepherd; there is nothing I lack." In the course of Israelite history, we come across many references to Yahweh as the shepherd and Israel as his flock of sheep, but none is more moving than the long discourse in chapter thirty-four of Ezekiel.

In this famous prophecy, Yahweh first of all condemns the shepherds for pasturing themselves: "Woe to the shepherds of Israel who have been pasturing themselves. Should not shepherds, rather, pasture sheep?" (Ezek 34:2). Then, in Ezekiel 34:10, he says that he will remove those shepherds:

> Thus says the Lord God: I swear I am coming against these shepherds. I will claim my sheep from them and put a stop to their shepherding my sheep so that they may no longer pasture themselves.

Then, in Ezekiel 34:11-12, Yahweh promises that he himself will shepherd his flock:

> For thus says the Lord God: I myself will look after and tend my sheep. As a shepherd tends his flock when he finds himself among his scattered sheep, so will I tend my sheep.

Finally, in Ezekiel 34:23-24, he promises to set one shepherd over them:

> I will appoint one shepherd over them to pasture them, my servant David; he shall pasture them and be their shepherd. I, the Lord, will be their God, and my servant David shall be prince among them.

Later, in John 10, when Jesus boldly claims to be that good shepherd and son of David and to describe further how he will pasture his flock, his disciples will believe him. Let me quote John 10:11, 14-16:

> I am the good shepherd. A good shepherd lays down his life for the sheep. . . . I am the good shepherd, and I know mine and mine know me, just as the Father knows me and I know the Father; and I will lay down my life for the sheep. I have other sheep that do not belong to this fold. These also I must lead, and they will hear my voice, and there will be one flock, one shepherd.

However, like his Father, Jesus is not yet finished when he promises to shepherd the sheep himself. He will not always be among us in a visible way, so he appoints another to shepherd his flock. First, he extracts from Simon Peter a three-fold declaration of love to make up for Peter's denying him three times during his passion. Then, in 21:15-17, he tells Peter: "Feed my lambs. . . . Tend my sheep. . . . Feed my sheep." What could be clearer? No wonder Peter says what he does to those whom the apostles had chosen as presbyters (bishops or priests) in 1 Peter 5:2-4:

> Tend the flock of God in your midst, [overseeing] not by constraint but willingly, as God would have it, not for shameful profit but eagerly. Do not Lord it over those assigned to you, but be examples to the flock. And when the chief Shepherd is revealed, you will receive the unfolding crown of glory.

The image of the shepherd and his sheep is indeed a true picture of God in his loving relationship with us humans. When we stop to think about it, it would have been difficult to find a more suitable symbol. We are indeed like sheep, dumb and dirty, depending solely on our shepherd to feed us (at least by leading us to good pasture), to water us (at least by guiding us to living streams), and to patch up our wounds. All of this is to be done in a spirit of faithful love and gentle caring for the sheep.

But I cannot help noticing that the very next Sunday, which is the Fifth Sunday of Easter, the gospel reading for the "B" cycle is John 15:1-8 about the true vine and its branches, leading on the next Sunday to all three of the gospel readings speaking of love and intimacy in our relationship with God. Let us leave that Sixth Sunday for the moment and dwell on the true vine and its branches.

In the entire gospel of John, there are only two formal parables in which Jesus says, "I am the good Shepherd" and "I am the true vine." And, providentially, in the Old Testament, there is a single psalm that contains both symbols: Psalm 80. In verses 2-4, the psalm speaks of the shepherd:

> Shepherd of Israel, listen,
> > Guide of the flock of Joseph!
> From your throne upon the cherubim reveal
> > to yourself Ephraim, Benjamin, and Manasseh.

> Stir up your power, come to save us.
> O Lord of hosts, restore us;
>> Let your face shine upon us,
>> That we may be saved.

References to the vine are in Psalm 80:9-12:

> You brought a vine out of Egypt;
>> You drove away the nations and planted it.
> You cleared the ground;
>> It *took root* and filled the land.
> The mountains were covered by its shadow,
>> the cedars of God by its branches.
> It sent out boughs as far as the sea,
>> shoots as far as the river.

Yes, both these great figures, the good shepherd and the true vine, are found in the one Psalm 80. Of course, they are more developed in the New Testament than in the Old. In the New Testament, Jesus, our Good Shepherd, knows us, leads us, and lays down his life for us that we may have life "and have it more abundantly" (John 10:10). In the New Testament, Jesus is the True Vine and "whoever remains in me and I in him will bear much fruit, because without me you can do nothing" (John 15:5).

The gospel readings for all three cycles of the Sixth Sunday of Easter are full of meaning: first, from the gospel reading for the "A" cycle, John 14:21 gives us the following:

> Whoever has my commandments and observes them is the one who loves me. And whoever loves me will be loved by my Father, and I will love him and reveal myself to him.

Then, from the gospel reading for the "C" cycle, we read in John 14:23:

> Whoever loves me will keep my word, and my Father will love him, and we will come to him and make our dwelling with him.

Finally, from the gospel reading for the "B" cycle in what is obviously a continuation of the thought of the previous Sunday, we read in John 15:12-15:

> This is my commandment: love one another as I love you.
> No one has greater love than this, to lay down one's life for
> one's friends. You are my friends if you do what I command
> you. I no longer call you slaves, because a slave does not
> know what his master is doing. I have called you friends,
> because I have told you everything I have heard from my
> Father.

These are key references in the story of Jesus' love for us, references that deserve to be read and re-read in order for us to derive the depth of meaning intended by John and Our Blessed Savior. Obviously, they are also extremely important to our personal spiritual growth.

Ascension

On the Thursday after the Sixth Sunday of the Easter season, we celebrate the Feast of the Ascension—the last day on which Jesus appeared on the earth, the day on which, in the Lucan tradition at least, Jesus ascended bodily to take his place at the right hand of God, the Father. It is a great feast of Jesus, a holy day of obligation in many parts of the world.

For that reason, it is important that we take a good look at the liturgy of the feast in order to understand its depth of meaning. Remember that Jesus, in his incarnation, took upon himself our spirit and our flesh. Taking on our flesh meant he took on our human nature at its weakest—subject to sickness, injury, death, temptation, and sin. In Jesus' case, we are assured in Hebrews 4:15 that:

> We do not have a high priest who is unable to sympathize
> with our weaknesses, but one who has similarly been tested
> in every way, yet without sin.

Jesus lived, suffered, died for our sins, and rose for our justification; it remained for Jesus, having fulfilled all that was expected of him in his obedience to his Father, to take his rightful place, as God and man, in heaven with the Father. What a triumph that must have been for our human nature. Having probed the depths of degradation in our human nature, it was time to explore the heights in that same human nature. Indeed, what a triumph and challenge it is for us to pass through this life faithfully that we may rejoice with Jesus in his triumph.

However, a particular challenge remains: When does our bodily resurrection take place? Are we destined to join Jesus in his ascension only on the Last Day (in Greek, the *éschaton* or *paroúsia*). This has been the common belief of Christians down through the centuries, but is it truly a belief or is it simply the result of traditional dependence on Greek philosophy? In Hebrew anthropology which is that of the Bible as well, we are not just body and soul, but flesh, person, and spirit. In fact, the word for "person" or "being" (Hebrew *nephesh*) is usually translated into Greek by the word for "body" (*sôma*) or "soul" (*psychê*). The Hebrew mentality could never have pictured a person in the next life without a body. Hence, I believe—subject to higher judgment—that when we die, we receive a new body. I believe that St. Paul is saying the same thing in 1 Corinthians 15 and 2 Corinthians 5. The way in which we differ from Jesus and Mary is that Jesus rose from the dead and ascended into heaven and Mary was assumed into heaven, both of whom with the self-same bodies with which they lived this life. We do not have that privilege, but we receive the next-best gift, whole new bodies. Thus we are able to continue a personal existence in the next life, for a soul without a body is not a person.

Now, let us look at the Scriptures involved. In the first reading, we have the story of the ascension as we see it in Acts 1:1-11. These verses give Jesus the opportunity to provide the outline of Acts. When the apostles desire to know when he plans to restore the kingdom to Israel, he answers:

> It is not for you to know the times or seasons that the Father has established by his own authority. But you will receive power when the Holy Spirit comes upon you, and you will be my witnesses in Jerusalem, throughout Judea and Samaria, and to the ends of the earth.

The Second Reading is from Ephesians 1:17-23 which is rich in the gifts given to Christ by the resurrection and ascension and, through him, to all who are united with him:

> [I pray] that the God of our Lord Jesus Christ, the Father of glory, may give you a spirit of wisdom and revelation resulting in knowledge of him. May the eyes of [your] hearts

be enlightened, that you may know what is the hope that belongs to his call, what are the riches of glory in his inheritance among the holy ones, and what is the surpassing greatness of his power for us who believe, in accord with the exercise of his great might, which he worked in Christ, raising him from the dead and seating him at his right hand in the heavens, far above every principality, authority, power, and dominion, and every name that is named not only in this age but also in the one to come. And he put all things beneath his feet and gave him as head over all things to the church, which is his body, the fullness of the one who fills all things in every way.

The gospel reading varies according to the cycle, Matthew 28:16-20 for cycle "A" being the great commission given to the apostles by Christ:

The eleven disciples went to Galilee, to the mountain to which Jesus had ordered them. When they saw him, they worshiped, but they doubted. Then Jesus approached and said to them, "All power in heaven and on earth has been given to me. Go, therefore, and make disciples of all nations, baptizing them in the name of the Father, and of the Son, and of the holy Spirit, teaching them to observe all that I have commanded you. And behold, I am with you always, until the end of the age."

It is legitimate for us to ask *how* he is with us. The answer is comforting: Christ is with us in the Church, in the Scriptures, and in each one of us as he continues his life and ministry through us. What a challenge of evangelization is given to us in this final commission to the apostles and the entire Church.

The "B" cycle uses part of the longer ending from Mark:

He said to them, "Go into the whole world and proclaim the gospel to every creature. Whoever believes and is baptized will be saved; whoever does not believe will be condemned. These signs will accompany those who believe: in my name they will drive out demons, they will speak new languages. They will pick up serpents [with their hands], and if they drink any deadly thing, it will not harm them. They will lay hands on the sick, and they will recover." So then the Lord Jesus, after he spoke to them, was taken up

> into heaven and took his seat at the right hand of God. But
> they went forth and preached everywhere, while the Lord
> worked with them and confirmed the word through accom-
> panying signs (16:15-20).

The "C" cycle uses the conclusion of the Gospel of Luke:

> And he said to them, "Thus it is written that the Messiah
> would suffer and rise from the dead on the third day and
> that repentance, for the forgiveness of sins, would be
> preached in his name to all the nations, beginning from
> Jerusalem. You are witnesses of these things. And [behold]
> I am sending the promise of my Father upon you, but stay
> in the city until you are clothed with power from on high."
> Then he led them [out] as far as Bethany, raised his hands,
> and blessed them. As he blessed them he parted from them
> and was taken up to heaven. They did him homage and then
> returned to Jerusalem with great joy, and they were continu-
> ally in the temple praising God (24:46-53).

Such is the conclusion of the ascension of Jesus. My readers
will have noted how varied are the endings of the gospels read
on the ascension as gospel readings. Of course, the endings
of John's Gospel are just as varied. What that says to me is
that each human author, inspired by God, wrote in given cir-
cumstances and according to his own genius. The greatest
crime in biblical circles would be for someone to weave the four
accounts into one story for popular usage; then, the individual flavor of each gospel would be lost. This is generally done
automatically at Christmas when the events of the two "infancy" gospels of Matthew and Luke are woven together. Perhaps that is excusable at Christmas time, but for study of the
gospels it is best to keep them separate.

Pentecost

We come now to the final feast of the Easter season, and a
most beautiful and important feast it is. In fact, it is much more
than we normally celebrate. Most Catholics do not realize that
Pentecost was a Jewish feast long before it became a Christian
celebration. Fifty days after their departure from slavery in
Egypt, the Israelites arrive at Mount Sinai where they are in-

vited to enter into a covenant relationship with Yahweh. In some of the most memorable language of the Old Testament, Yahweh says to Moses in Exodus 19:3-6:

> Thus shall you say to the house of Jacob; tell the Israelites: "You have seen for yourselves how I treated the Egyptians and how I bore you up on eagle wings and brought you here to myself. Therefore, if you hearken to my voice and keep my covenant, you shall be my special possession, dearer to me than all other people, though all the earth is mine. You shall be to me a kingdom of priests, a holy nation." That is what you must tell the Israelites.

What a tender, gentle invitation to a covenant relationship without—did you notice?—one word about law or precepts. Those are given in the following chapter where the Ten Commandments are first listed; there they are the conditions or specifications of the covenant. All the other laws, over six hundred of them, were drawn up in the course of Israelite history and put back into the Torah the way we add amendments to our own constitution. They were reducible to the Ten Commandments, the means of keeping the covenant.

Unfortunately, by the time Jesus came among us, our Jewish brethren had largely abandoned the covenant for the Law, especially the law of Sabbath rest. Did you ever notice how often Jesus deliberately did things forbidden on the Sabbath? As he himself said in Mark 2:27-28:

> The sabbath was made for man, not man for the sabbath. That is why the Son of Man is lord even of the sabbath!

When he was asked which was the greatest commandment of the law, he chose the commandment to love God in Deuteronomy 6:4-5 and the commandment to love our neighbor as ourselves in Leviticus 19:18 because these two commandments are precepts of love and relationship, not just the fulfilling of a law. He himself tried to draw his fellow Jews back into a covenant relationship with his Father by his personal appeal in Matthew 11:28-30:

> Come to me, all you who labor and are burdened [under all these laws imposed by man], and I will give you rest. Take

> my yoke [my law, my covenant relationship] upon you and
> learn from me, for I am meek and humble of heart; and you
> will find rest for yourselves. For my yoke is easy, and my
> burden light.

Finally, having "loved his own in the world . . ., he loved
them to the end" (John 13:1). In his great love for us, he initiated a new covenant when he said at the Last Supper:

> This cup is the new covenant in my blood, which will be shed
> for you (Luke 22:20).

We are all initiated into this covenant relationship with him
by our baptism. That is why Peter in his First Letter which is
generally regarded by Scripture scholars as a kind of baptismal homily, declares in 1 Peter 2:9:

> But you are "a chosen race, a royal priesthood, a holy na-
> tion, a people of his own, so that you may announce the
> praises" of him who called you out of darkness into his won-
> derful light.

As a consequence of our "royal priesthood," we should look
upon Pentecost as a special time to renew our covenant relationship; we should celebrate every Mass as a renewal of our
covenant relationship; and we should regard the covenant relationship with God as our preparation for the unending relationship with God in Heaven. For this reason Acts 2:1 begins,
"When the time for Pentecost was fulfilled. . . ."

Next, Pentecost is preeminently a time of prayer, as evidenced by the Scripture notice in Acts 1:13-14:

> When they entered the city they went to the upper room
> where they were staying, Peter and John and James and An-
> drew, Philip and Thomas, Bartholomew and Matthew, James
> son of Alphaeus, Simon the Zealot, and Judas son of James.
> All these devoted themselves with one accord to prayer, to-
> gether with some women, and Mary the mother of Jesus,
> and his brothers.

The period between the feast of the Ascension of Jesus and
Pentecost is generally considered to be the time when the

Church devoted itself to its first novena because it lasted exactly nine days and was given over to prayer. We can leave the answer to what kind of prayer—petition or mental prayer, active or passive contemplation—to the Holy Spirit. As St. Paul says in Romans 8:26-27:

> In the same way, the Spirit too comes to the aid of our weakness; for we do not know how to pray as we ought, but the Spirit itself intercedes with inexpressible groanings. And the one who searches hearts knows what is the intention of the Spirit, because it intercedes for the holy ones according to God's will.

This emphasis on prayer is also indicated in the Liturgy. In the gospel reading for the Sunday between Ascension and Pentecost, which is the Seventh Sunday of Easter, all three cycles of readings carry that most eloquent of all prayers, the high-priestly prayer of Jesus for his followers in John 17.

Besides the covenant and prayer, Pentecost is a time of special personal growth in the life of the spirit. Let us listen again to Paul in Romans 8:14-17:

> For those who are led by the Spirit of God are children of God. For you did not receive a spirit of slavery to fall back into fear, but you received a spirit of adoption, through which we cry, ''*Abba*, Father!'' The Spirit itself bears witness with our spirit that we are children of God, and if children, then heirs, heirs of God and joint heirs with Christ, if only we suffer with him so that we may also be glorified with him.

It is also a time of community building, for that is what Mary and the apostles were doing in the Upper Room where they awaited the Holy Spirit. Of course, the painful pitting of Jew against Greek, noticeable even in the sixth chapter of Acts, continued on throughout early Christianity. Nonetheless, community building is extremely important for the New Testament mind, and that is why Acts 1:15 states parenthetically, ''there was a group of about one hundred and twenty persons in the one place,'' the number one hundred twenty being sufficient to justify the building of a synagogue.

So far we have been studying the meaning of Pentecost before the descent of the Holy Spirit, and we have seen that

Pentecost was important as a covenant feast, as a time of prayer, and as a time of community building. Now let us take up its significance to the Christian with the coming of the Holy Spirit.

First of all, we have the outward signs of Pentecost: "a noise like a strong driving wind" and the tongues of fire which "parted and came to rest on each one of them" (Acts 2:2-3). The mighty wind is a reminder of Genesis 1:2, where "a mighty wind swept over the waters." Here it symbolizes the creative spirit of God. The "parted tongues" serve as an extraordinary teaching tool about spiritual gifts, as Paul so beautifully describes in 1 Corinthians 12:4-7:

> There are different kinds of spiritual gifts but the same Spirit; there are different forms of service but the same Lord; there are different workings but the same God who produces all of them in everyone. To each individual the manifestation of the Spirit is given for some benefit.

The most evident result of the coming of the Holy Spirit was that now the apostles were able to speak in various languages without the need to study them. This was the "gift of tongues" which astonished their hearers. In fact, it continues to astonish hearers and for that may God be praised! But I am afraid that this gift has been used in the past for self-glorification and elitism. (Read Paul in chapters 12-14 of 1 Corinthians). It is significant to me that, while Paul places the gift of tongues last in his list of gifts in 1 Corinthians 12:27-28, in his other two lists of the gifts (Romans 12:6-8, Ephesians 4:11-13), he omits this gift altogether. Nor is there any evidence that Jesus himself ever used the gift of tongues.

But for the apostles on Pentecost, the gift of tongues had the desired effect. It transformed the babel of disputing tongues found in Genesis 11:1-9 into understandable speech and supplied a new hope for unity in the world. The Holy Spirit, by his gift of tongues, got the people's attention and gave St. Peter the opportunity to explain the *kérygma* to the disparate Jews so that, on the same day, three thousand souls were added to the Church.

In addition to the charismatic gifts given for the service of others, the Holy Spirit, more importantly, confers the gifts of the spirit, which are sanctifying and are listed in Isaiah 11:2: wisdom, understanding, knowledge, counsel, fortitude, piety, and fear of the Lord. These attributes are ascribed to the Messiah when he appears among us. Therefore, the right to confer the gifts of the spirit is part of the Spirit's marvelous ability to transform us into Jesus Christ. This is his greatest role, to be an ever-present mediator or, perhaps better still, moderator who possesses the power, little by little and almost without our knowing, to change us radically into the risen Christ.

Let us take a quick look at the Scripture readings chosen for the feast of Pentecost so that we may discern how they confirm what we have been talking about. For example, in the Pentecost vigil Mass, there is a choice of four readings: Genesis 11:1-9, about the tower of Babel and the confusion of languages (the deeper lesson being that human beings cannot build their own way to heaven, they must wait on God's initiative as happens in the next chapter with the call of Abram); Exodus 19:3-8a, 16-20b, about the covenant between Yahweh and Israel; Ezekiel 37:1-14, about the dry bones—symbolizing Israel without spirit—which reunite and stand once the spirit comes among them; and Joel 3:1-5, which deserves to be quoted in full:

> Then afterward I will pour out my spirit upon all mankind.
> Your sons and daughters shall prophecy, your old men
> shall dream dreams, your young men shall see visions;
> Even upon the servants and the handmaids, in those days,
> I will pour out my spirit. And I will work wonders
> in the heavens and on the earth,
> blood, fire, and columns of smoke;
> The sun will be turned to darkness, and the moon to blood,
> At the coming of the day of the Lord, the great and
> terrible day. Then eveyone shall be rescued who
> calls on the name of the Lord;
> For on Mount Zion there shall be a remnant, as the Lord
> has said, And in Jerusalem survivors whom the Lord
> shall call.

The responsorial psalm is Psalm 104, while the second reading is from Romans 8:22-27, especially about prayer. The gospel reading is from John 7:37-39:

> On the last and greatest day of the feast [Tabernacles?], Jesus stood up and exclaimed, "Let anyone who thirsts come to me and drink. Whoever believes in me, as scripture says: 'Rivers of living water will flow from within him.' " He said this in reference to the Spirit that those who came to believe in him were to receive. There was, of course, no Spirit yet, because Jesus had not yet been glorified.

The Scripture readings for the feast of Pentecost itself are as follows: the first reading is taken from Acts 2:1-11 and contains the actual account of the descent of the Holy Spirit and the results thereof; the responsorial psalm is a repetition of Psalm 104; the second reading is taken from 1 Corinthians 12:3b-7, 12-13, referring to the many charismatic gifts varying greatly from person to person, yet all coming from the one Spirit; and the gospel reading is from John 20:19-23, which I will quote in full:

> On the evening of that first day of the week, when the doors were locked, where the disciples were, for fear of the Jews, Jesus came and stood in their midst and said to them, "Peace be with you." When he had said this, he showed them his hands and his side. The disciples rejoiced when they saw the Lord. [Jesus] said to them again, "Peace be with you. As the Father has sent me, so I send you." And when he had said this, he breathed on them and said to them, "Receive the Holy Spirit. Whose sins you forgive are forgiven them, and whose sins you retain are retained."

We have now come to the conclusion of the Easter season. Tomorrow begins Ordinary Time II. As we have seen, this season is rich in its Scripture readings, reflecting the abundance of flowers of every kind that characterize this Holy season. Let us not let any of these precious blossoms go to waste; let us rather guard them gently, but firmly, for the harvest at the end.

5 ORDINARY TIME II

We have now arrived at the long period of Ordinary Time that follows upon the Easter season. As I mentioned earlier, time is never ordinary, for it is the stuff of our eternity, the fabric of our forever. Since this is the final episode of our study of the Church year and there are a number of solemnities and feasts, it behoves me to merely hit the highlights, enough for my readers to immerse themselves in the liturgy of Ordinary Time II.

It is important to bear in mind that Ordinary Time II, according to the nature of things, is hardly to be regarded as one of the principal episodes of the liturgical year. But if we pause a moment to realize that—between the blossoms of Easter and the full maturing of the fruit at the end of the harvest—there must be a certain amount of time for the process of ripening and aging, then we derive a new and added regard for Ordinary Time II.

The material for the Sundays of Ordinary Time II is made up of two things: the largely focused use of Scriptures to mark successively the ordinary times as they occur, and the succession of special solemnities and feasts that punctuate the time and give it substance. If the Scripture readings form the background music, then the solemnities and feasts provide the melody. If the readings form the ferns, then the solemnities and feasts provide the flowers that add color to the ferns. Let us examine each of them in turn.

Looking at the Sunday gospel readings, it is easy for us to grasp that Matthew is used in cycle ''A,'' Mark in cycle ''B,'' and Luke in cycle ''C.'' But there is one important exception. Beginning with the Seventeenth Sunday in Ordinary Time (approximately midway through the season of Ordinary Time), in place of Mark we have John Six, the Eucharistic discourse of Jesus, in the Gospel readings; Mark returning in the Twenty-second Sunday and continuing until the Thirty-Fourth or Last Sunday of the year (Christ the King) when we again encounter John.

The first readings will be taken from any of the books, primarily of the Old Testament, to match the gospel readings. The responsorial psalms are chosen to follow the line of thought in the first readings. And the second or intermediate reading is a continuous one from the New Testament without any attempt to match the other two readings.

So much for the Sundays of Ordinary Time II. During the weekdays the Gospel of Mark covers the first nine weeks of Ordinary Time; Matthew continues until the Twenty-first week; and Luke completes the remainder of the Church year. During this same period of time, Paul's Letters are favored as the first reading, in a continuous fashion, although Samuel, Kings, Genesis, and other books of the Old Testament are used in alternate years as the first readings. Of course, the responsorial psalm is chosen to fit the first reading. This rapid and scant description of the Scripture readings for Ordinary Time II of the Church year hardly does justice to the care with which these segments must have been chosen, but it will have to do, simply because the type of book that we are attempting to write does not permit any other.

Let us go on, then, to the solemnities and feasts that occur during Ordinary Time II and give direction to the time of summer and fall, seasons which occur during this period.

Holy Trinity

The first and greatest of solemnities, one which occurs just a week after Pentecost, is that of the Most Holy Trinity. In a true sense, this great feast includes all the rest, although its inclusion now seems somewhat late in the Church year. Every Sunday is a celebration of the Holy Trinity, for as I explained earlier, God began creation on the first day of the week, Jesus rose from the dead on the first day of the week, and the Holy Spirit descended upon the new Church on the first day of the week. However, in the course of time, it seemed that there should be a special feast in honor of the Holy Trinity, so it was added in 1334 by Pope John XXII who ordered it to be celebrated on the First Sunday after Pentecost. However, it was not until 1911 that it was raised from a feast to a solemnity.

The Scripture readings for the solemnity of the Holy Trinity are threefold and are designed to help us believe in and stand in awe of this great mystery. Indeed, we do stand in awe. But is that what God wants of us? If the heart of religion is our relationship with God, then how can we possibly be content only to believe in and stand in awe before him? There must be more that we can do.

We can relate to the Son because he became human like us. We can relate to the Father because we have all had earthly fathers, good or bad, abusive or sensitive, who can help us to relate to God Our Father as a father. But how can we relate to the Holy Spirit in our lives? Only by living the life of the spirit can we truly relate to the movements of the Holy Spirit.

There is still another way in which we can relate to the three persons of the Holy Trinity. It is important to note that, outside of the ending of Matthew's Gospel and a few greetings and farewells from Paul, the Sacred Scriptures do not invite us to relate to the whole Trinity, but rather to each individual person of the Trinity in much the same way that they relate to each other. We refer to St. Augustine's famous saying from his *Confessions*, ''Thou hast made us for thyself, O Lord, and our hearts are restless until they rest in thee.''[1] If God has made us for himself, is it not possible that a relationship with each of the persons of the Trinity would fulfill a deep personal need within us?

I am not considering here our personal need for food, clothing, and housing, which we all need, but the more non-material needs that are less obvious. For example, my deepest personal need is for *identity*. I need to know who and what I am. After studying every book in the library on self-image and self-respect, I must return to Genesis 1:27 and Romans

---

1. St. Augustine, *The Confessions of Saint Augustine,* trans. F. J. Sheed (New York: Sheed & Ward, 1943) 3.

8:29 to realize that Christ is my image and that my entire goal in life is to be as much like Jesus Christ as possible.

We human beings have a second basic need—*security*. We thought we would feel more secure at the end of the Cold War, but quite the opposite seems to be true. The Cold War, with its two adversaries, has given way to fierce tribal warfare which we find impossible to understand. Apart from war, the complexity of life and the lure of hypertechnology are a great source of people's lack of self-esteem. What are we to do? Where does our salvation lie? It rests precisely where Jesus says it does in the Sermon on the Mount (Matt 6:25-34): in our complete trust in God as our Father, our ''Daddy,'' which is the meaning of the familiar Aramaic term *''Abba''* that Jesus alone used (Mark 14:36) but which we also are invited to use (Rom 8:15; Gal 4:6).

Finally, I have a third basic personal need for *direction* in my life. What shall I do? What should I become? We can plan the course of our life as fully as possible, but when we want to know in what direction to develop, we have the Holy Spirit given us by the Father and the Son to direct us.

We see, then, how important it is for us to constantly strive to know each person of the Trinity clearly, to love each one dearly, and to relate to each one fully. Only thus will we grow in our personal spiritual lives. Only thus will the solemnity of the Holy Trinity become for us a delicate flower which is the promise of personal growth.

Corpus Christi

The feast of Corpus Christi (Body of Christ) is the second great solemnity that we find during Ordinary Time II. It is centered on the Eucharist and its importance to our daily spiritual growth. Since I spoke at some length about the Eucharist when I first began, I invite the reader to review what I have said there. However, since the Holy Eucharist is perhaps the greatest means of our salvation, we need to take a close look at the Scripture readings for the day and carefully consider some other matters of great importance.

The feast of Corpus Christi was celebrated in Rome soon after it was first celebrated at Liege, Belgium in 1247. Providentially,

Pope Urban IV had served earlier as archdeacon of Liege, so it was a simple matter for him to bring the feast to Rome. So it was, then, that Pope Urban IV extended the feast to the whole Church in 1264. However, it did not succeed in being firmly established until new decrees were issued by Pope Clement V at the Council of Vienne in 1311–1312 and by Pope John XXII in 1317. The role of Thomas Aquinas in devising propers for this Mass is disputed.

The Scripture readings for this particular Holy Eucharist are threefold and extremely rich. For the "A" cycle, the first reading is from Deuteronomy 8:2-3, 14b–16a; a summary of the wanderings in the desert. The responsorial psalm is from Psalm 147. The second reading is from 1 Corinthians 10:16-17, pertaining to the Eucharist. The gospel is from John 6:51-59, Jesus' promise of the Eucharist. The "B" cycle is very interesting. The first reading is from Exodus 24:3-8, ratification of the covenant; the responsorial psalm is the beautiful Psalm 116; the second reading is from Hebrews 9:11-15 on the new covenant; and the gospel reading is the institution of the Eucharist in Mark 12:16, 22-26.

For the "C" cycle, the first reading is Melchisedech's blessing of Abram in Genesis 14:18-20; the responsorial psalm is Psalm 110, in which the Messiah is called a priest forever according to the order of Melchisedech; the second reading is the institution of the Eucharist in 1 Corinthians 11:23-26; and the gospel reading is the multiplication of the loaves of bread and fishes from Luke 9:11b-17.

As stimulating as the Scripture readings may be, it seems to me that here, as with the feast of the Trinity, the principal effects of the feast will occur from our actually celebrating it. Of course, since it normally gets transferred to the nearest Sunday these days, our chances of actually participating in the ritual for the rest of Corpus Christi are better than ever.

Earlier, I spoke at some length about the Eucharist in the form of the Holy Sacrifice of the Mass. But I would like to add here a small commentary on the reservation of the Blessed Sacrament. The Second Vatican Council and other decrees were correct in recommmending that the Blessed Sacrament be kept on a side altar or in a side chapel, and I applaud their wisdom. But it seems to me imperative that there be some place where a person can stop in and speak with the Lord. Many, but not all, churches now reserve the Blessed Sacrament in a side chapel which is kept unlocked during the day. This is ideal. I cannot overstress the many graces that have come to me through the simple practice of never ignoring Jesus as I pass by on my way to some work or recreation.

Sacred Heart

Third in a row of solemnities which occur one after the other during Ordinary Time II is the feast of the Sacred Heart. If Corpus Christi is observed on the Thursday after the feast of the Holy Trinity—or the following Sunday where it is not a holy day of obligation—then the Feast of the Sacred Heart is observed the following Friday.

Devotion to the Sacred Heart was promoted by medieval mystics such as St. Gertrude (1256–1301), later by the Jesuits using such texts as John 7:37 and 19:34. In seventeenth-century France, devotion to the Sacred Heart was spread zealously by St. John Eudes, a French Oratorian, who is one of the most underrated of saints. Finally, thanks largely to the visions of the Sacred Heart by St. Margaret Mary Alacoque, a Visitation nun, the feast was added to the general calendar in 1856 and celebrated the Friday after the octave of Corpus Christi. In 1889, it was made a solemnity.

The Scripture readings for the feast of the Sacred Heart are all very instructive and moving. In cycle "A," we find for the first reading Deuteronomy 7:6-11: Moses' reminder to the people of Israel that God chose them simply because he loved them. The responsorial psalm is Psalm 103. The second reading is from 1 John 4:7-16, on the beauty of divine love; and the gospel reading is the "Johannine" section of Matthew, chapter eleven, verses twenty-five to thirty.

The readings for cycle "B" are equally impressive. The first is from the prophet of divine love, Hosea 11:1a, 3-4, 8c-9. The responsorial psalm is Isaiah 12:2-3, 4-6. The second reading is Paul's beautiful section on love in Ephesians 3:8-12, 14-19. The gospel reading recalls the piercing of Jesus' heart after his death in John 19:31-37.

Cycle "C" emphasizes the identity of the Sacred Heart and Jesus, the Good Shepherd. The first reading is from Ezekiel 34:11-16, the responsorial psalm from Psalm 23. The second reading is on the love of God for us in Romans 5:5-11. The gospel reading is about the lost sheep, the first of the three about those who are lost, in Luke 15:3-7.

It is significant that not only the feast itself but all of June is dedicated to the Sacred Heart and that all through the year we are encouraged to say the votive Mass of the Sacred Heart on the first Friday of each month. This is a moving feast. It honors incarnate love, the love of God-made-man for us. It also honors, though in a secondary way, the pain Jesus felt, knowing that his sacrifice would be in vain, knowing that many if not most of those whom he loves and calls to greater love would turn a deaf ear and seek the tawdry pleasures of this world.

Assumption

After celebrating the solemnities of the Birthday of John the Baptist on June 24 and of Sts. Peter and Paul on June 29, and after honoring the feast of the Transfiguration of the Lord on August 6, we are ready to celebrate the beautiful solemnity of the Assumption of Mary. This seems to have been her earliest feast, for it is recorded in the Armenian Lectionary of the fifth century that a feast in honor of Mary the Mother of God (*theotókos*) was observed in Jerusalem on August 15. It became the principal feast of Mary throughout the Christian world.

The feast of the Assumption also has a vigil whose first reading is from 1 Chronicles 15:3-4, 15-16; 16:1-2 about the bringing of the ark of the covenant into Jerusalem in the time of David. The responsorial psalm continues the same thought in Psalm 132:6-7, 9-10, 13-14. The second reading is concerned with what Paul has to declare about resurrection in 1 Corinthians 15:54-57. And the gospel reading is the very short saying of Jesus in Luke 11:27-28: "Rather, blessed are those who hear the word of God and observe it."

For the feast of the Assumption itself, the readings are more appropriate. The first reading is about the woman clothed with the sun from Revelation 12:1-6a, 10ab, while the responsorial psalm is about the beauty of the queen in Psalm 45. The second reading is concerned with the resurrection in 1 Corinthians 15:20-26. Finally, the gospel reading comprises the visitation and succeeding *Magnificat* as found in Luke 1:39-56.

It may seem strange, in the middle of the summer, that we take time to celebrate the feast of the Assumption, but a little thought indicates the appropriateness of it. Here we are, growing from flower to fruit, spinning our wheels in the midst of late summer, much in need of a boost, and then we have it— Mary. What a boost she is to us in our spiritual wanderings. She has arrived; she is already in heaven. We are still on our way. In Wordsworth's sonnet on the Virgin, she is "our tainted nature's solitary boast"[2] while we are beset with temptations of every kind.

If ever there was a time when we needed her help around us, it is at this juncture of our lives. Her feast exists as a reminder that she is always there for us, particularly in our most trying times. All we need to do is reach out to her and accept her maternal love. She is our mother, our model, our mentor.

All Saints

Having celebrated the feasts of the Beheading of John the Baptist (August 29), the Birthday of Mary (September 8), the Exaltation of the Cross (September 14), and Sts. Michael, Gabriel, and Raphael (September 29), we are now ready for the feast of All Saints on November 1. When we stop to think about it, we find that this feast is particularly appropriate at this time. We have been enduring and experiencing the long journey to our heavenly Jerusalem. We have felt the flowers way back at the time of Easter, and now we are in the midst of this long season of Ordinary Time II, reaching toward the harvest at the end of November. What a relief, then, to remember in this feast of All Saints our parents, brothers, and sisters who may have gone before us to their heavenly reward. What

2. William Wordsworth, "The Virgin," *The Poems*, vol. 2, ed. John O. Hayden (New Haven, Ct.: Yale University Press, 1981) 474.

encouragement they give us. How they keep our eyes fixed on Christ in fulfillment of what Paul tells us in Philippians 3:13-14:

> Just one thing: forgetting what lies behind but straining forward to what lies ahead, I continue my pursuit toward the goal, the prize of God's upward calling, in Christ Jesus.

In the Roman Church, observance of the feast of All Saints on November 1 is placed in the ninth century. In the Greek church, All Saints Day was commemorated on the first Sunday after Pentecost since the fourth century. Early in the seventh century, Pope Boniface IV consecrated the Pantheon in Rome as the Church of Santa Maria ad Martyres. Pope Gregory IV (827-844) petitioned Emperor Louis the Pious, son of the great Charlemagne, to observe the feast on November 1 throughout the new Holy Roman Empire. The vigil of All Saints Day, known in England as All Hallows Eve or Halloween, was abolished in 1955.

The Readings for All Saints Day are especially well-chosen. The first reading is from Revelation 7:2-4, 9-14 and depicts the vision of "a great multitude, which no one could count, from every nation, race, people, and tongue" standing before the throne of God and crying, "Salvation comes from our God, who is seated on the throne, and from the Lamb." The responsorial psalm is taken from Psalm 24. The second reading is the beautiful one from 1 John 3:1-3, about which I have already commented. And the gospel reading features the beatitudes of the Sermon on the Mount in Matthew 5:1-12a.

All Souls

It may come as a surprise to some people that I include the feast of All Souls, or simply All Souls Day, among the great feasts providing flowers of inspiration and encouragement to us on our journey. After all, it is a source of embarrassment to those of us in apologetics because there is no mention of purgatory in the Bible. But, realistically, it is to be expected that most of us will undergo some purification before we are ready to enter complete heavenly bliss. As a matter of fact, I see the living presence of God himself as the burning sensation in this purification process. How long will it take? Who knows. It is appropriate for us to pray for the dead that they may be freed from their sins and be purified, for twice we read in the Book of Revelation that "nothing unclean will enter [the heavenly Jerusalem]" (Rev 21:26. See also 22:3).

The celebration of All Souls Day on November 2 dates from the year 998 when St. Odilo of Cluny ordered that prayers for all the dead be offered on that day. The practice spread rapidly in northern Europe, but Rome did not adopt it until the fourteenth century. The custom of offering three Masses for the dead began in Spain, was approved for that country in 1748, but did not win general approval until 1915 when Benedict XV extended it to all the world.

One of the reasons why this feast is important, especially in our time, is the pervasive and growing fear of death and the desire to cling to this life. However, when we look at life through the eyes of faith, our life really begins only when we die. This life, no matter how long it lasts, is like the nine months in the womb compared to a long and happy life after birth. If we could ask a fetus in the womb if it wanted to be born, it would probably say "No!" It is comfortable, secure, warm, and has all it needs to sustain life. Why go through the trauma of birth? But we cannot remain in the womb forever. So it is with death. The sooner we cease to look on death as the end of living and regard it as a birth to a new and truer life, the happier we will be. Birthdays are seldom celebrated in the Church year. Only the births of Jesus, John the Baptist, and Mary come to mind. The day of commemoration of the various saints is the date of their death, for that was the day of birth into eternity.

The choice of Scripture readings for today's Mass, unlike those of almost any other day, is left to the celebrant. Assuming that only one Mass is offered on this day—this has become more and more the practice since Vatican II—I will choose those readings which appeal to me. Someone else may be inclined to choose other readings.

For the first reading, therefore, I choose Wisdom 3:1-9, which speaks of the happiness of the just man who dies while those without faith counted his death a catastrophe. The responsorial psalm would be the ever-beautiful Psalm 23, ''The Lord is my shepherd; there is nothing I lack.''

For a second reading, I choose 2 Corinthians 5:1-10, which declares,

> For we know that if our earthly dwelling, a tent, should be destroyed, we have a building from God, a dwelling not made with hands, eternal in heaven.

For the gospel reading, I choose the raising of Lazarus in John 11:17-27, mainly because it contains, in dramatic fashion, all the elements of a theology of death and resurrection, particularly, Christ's words,

> I am the resurrection and the life; whoever believes in me, even if he dies, will live, and everyone who lives and believes in me will never die.

As we leave the penultimate feast before the end of the Church year, we feel some nostalgia, but mainly let us look toward the goal, ''the prize of God's upward calling, in Christ Jesus'' (Phil 3:14).

Christ the King

We come now to the final feast which closes the Church year, the feast of Christ the King. Pope Pius XI, in 1925, instituted this feast and commanded that it be celebrated on the last Sunday in October, just before All Saints Day. In 1969, it was moved to the more suitable place it now holds, bringing to a close the Church year.

Sometimes we tend to reject anything that is not a thousand years old, as if Christ is not still operating in and through the Church. It is not God's fault, but ours, that it took us so long to recognize the value of the liturgical year and of closing it with the feast of Christ the King. This is the perfect feast, representing the modern Catholic Church and comprising within itself everything that we look for in the closing feast of the Church year.

What is the purpose of the Church year? Is it not that Christ should reign both within and without our particular person? From his earliest steps until his last breath on Calvary, Christ's every thought concerned what he might do in order to achieve a lasting dominion over our hearts, our minds, our bodies, our souls, our spirits, so that he might reign over us without rival and continue his life and ministry through us.

On our part, there should be the greatest desire to have Jesus as our guest and as Lord over us. We are his possession. We are the sheep of his fold. We need to be under his benevolent rule. We need him to be King of our hearts, totally supreme in his rule over us.

That is precisely what this feast is about. It is not redundant, just another of too many feasts of Our Lord already in the Church calendar. No. It is a climactic one, the final feast of the Church year. Next week begins a new Church year. At this feast of Christ the King, we must ask ourselves whether or not he is the King of our heart, the King of our life.

The Scripture readings for this feast are carefully chosen and are threefold in design. The "A" cycle has, as its first reading and responsorial psalm, Ezekiel 34:11-12, 15-17 and Psalm 23. The second reading is from Paul's discourse on resurrection in 1 Corinthians 15:20-26b, 28, and the gospel reading is the grand general judgment of the sheep and goats by the Son of Man in Matthew 25:31-46. This cycle places strong emphasis on shepherding and sheep.

The "B" cycle emphasizes the kingship of Jesus. For the first reading, we see the Son of Man (Israel in the original meaning) in Daniel 7:13-14; the responsorial psalm is Psalm 93, one of the enthronement psalms. The second reading, which I will quote in full, is from Revelation 1:5-8:

> Jesus Christ [is] the faithful witness, the firstborn of the dead and ruler of the kings of the earth. To him who loves us and has freed us from our sins by his blood, who has made us into a kingdom, priests for his God and Father, to him be glory and power forever [and ever]. Amen.
> Behold, he is coming amid the clouds,
> and every eye will see him,
> even those who pierced him.

All the peoples of the earth will lament him.
Yes. Amen.
"I am the Alpha and the Omega," says the Lord God, "the
one who is and who was and who is to come, the almighty."

The gospel reading comprises the discussion of Pilate and Jesus
about kingship, which is recorded in the Rylands Papyrus, the
oldest fragment of the New Testament known to exist. In the
Bible it exists as John 18:33b-37.

The "C" cycle also stresses the kingship of Jesus. In the First
Reading, we have the submission of all Israel to David in 2
Samuel 5:1-3. The responsorial psalm is Psalm 122 which
speaks of the restoration of the lost tribes of Israel. In the sec-
ond reading, we have the beautiful passage about Jesus from
Colossians 1:12-20, which I will quote in full:

> [We give] thanks to the Father, who has made you fit to share
> in the inheritance of the holy ones in light. He delivered us
> from the power of darkness and transferred us to the king-
> dom of his beloved Son, in whom we have redemption, the
> forgiveness of sins.
> He is the image of the invisible God,
>   the firstborn of all creation.
> For in him were created all things
>   in heaven and on earth,
>   the visible and the invisible,
>   whether thrones or dominations
>   or principalities or powers;
>   all things were created through him
>   and for him.
> He is before all things,
>   and in him all things hold together.
> He is the head of the body, the church.
> He is the beginning, the firstborn from the dead,
> That in all things he himself might be preeminent.
> For in him all the fullness was pleased to dwell,
>   and through him to reconcile all things for him,
>   making peace by the blood of his cross. . . .

The gospel reading is taken from Luke 23:35-43 and contains
the two references to Jesus as King of the Jews: the first one
by the leaders with the people and the soldiers; the second

by the Good Thief, the sole voice contradicting them, who asks Jesus to remember him when he comes into his kingdom. Jesus replies, ''Amen, I say to you, today you will be with me in Paradise.''

Thus we bring to an end our treatment of the entire Church year. The feast of Christ the King is certainly the climax toward which the whole Church year is tending; therefore, it must be seen and interpreted within the context of the entire Church year, not just as a single feast occurring by itself. If we need to make any adjustments, then let them begin right away, for who knows the power of the Church year to enable us to grow in Jesus as we were destined to grow.

To complete this consideration of the Church year, I can think of nothing more apropos than the ''Song of Love,'' which I wrote many years ago but which is still relevant today:

Song of Love

Verse   Some men live only for riches,
        Some may live only for fame.
        My life is given to someone
        And Love is his name.

Chorus Love, how can I sing the rapture of
        Your charms,
        Your tenderness, Your fond caress.
      Love, how dare I e'er escape Your circling
        arms.
        The more I flee; the less I'm free.
        Once I dreamed that I might love another;
        Now I know there's only One for me.
        Unlike any ordinary lover,
        You'll be true to me throughout eternity.
        Now, though bitterness may come, I'll
        see it through,
        For at Your feet the bitter's sweet.
        And though weary, sick, and blind, I'll
        cling to You,
        You'll be my light, my very sight.
        Ah Love! You're life, and breath, and
        everything divine,
        And just to think, You're mine, all mine!

CONCLUSION

It is always a great pleasure to reach a conclusion and realize that our journey is coming to an end. However, in order for that conclusion to be valid and helpful, we must make an overview of the entire endeavor and try to present it to our readers as an organized whole that can be useful to them for their personal spiritual growth.

Beginning with Advent, when we are preparing for the coming of the Christ Child at Christmas, we have seen that this season is basically a time for plowing and harrowing the earth to render it suitable for the reception of the seed, the Word of God, inspired and incarnate. In this work, we receive great assistance from Mary—our Mother, Model, and Mentor—because we are called upon to celebrate two feasts in her honor. It is evident from the first feast that Mary has a real role in our personal spiritual life, especially in the importation of her three major contributions as seen from her responses to the Angel Gabriel: her humility, her purity, and her generous gift of love and self.

With the celebration of Christmas, we see that liturgy does not just look backward at the events which it has chosen to commemorate but basically takes what is past and brings it up to the present so that we may add our own contribution to it. It provides us with the great chance to add our own selves to the process. At Christmas, the seed is born in us which will grow into a great tree, and the birds of the air will come to nest in its branches.

After the celebration of Christmas, one of two special periods in the Church's year, we enjoy a brief period of what is regularly called Ordinary Time, although time is never ordinary because it is the stuff of our eternity. During the brief period of

Ordinary Time I, we see the beginning of the growth of the seed, the image of God, in our lives.

Then comes the great season of Lent, a time of weeding and pruning that growth of the special little plants. There is so much for us to weed and prune! The more seriously we do it, the more there appears for us to do. But only to the extent that we have weeded and pruned well, will we enjoy the flowers and fruit thereof.

Next comes the great Easter season, admittedly the greatest time of the entire Church year. Unfortunately, there is a discrepancy here. Although Christmas is second to Easter, it involves a baby, and we have many songs about it whereas Easter is concerned with a risen Lord, and has very few songs proper to it. We lack the experience to be able to relate to it validly. Basically, Easter marks the time of flowers, and there will be only as much fruit at the end of the season as we find flowers at Easter. Meanwhile, flowers help us to pass the time and enable us to bear things more calmly.

Following the great events of the Easter Triduum, we can then celebrate Easter itself, and thanks to the Church's hard work, the entire Easter season is a time when the Scriptures call us to God and his kingdom.

In the second period of Ordinary Time, called Ordinary Time II, we pass through the wild and unequal period between the flowering of Easter and the maturing of fruit at the end of the Church year. Here, the Scripture readings simply flow so that actually the feasts which occur during this time are more important than the time itself. The feasts of the Holy Trinity, of Corpus Christi, of the Sacred Heart, as well as the Assumption, All Saints, and All Souls prepare us for the great feast of Christ the King with which the liturgical year closes.

Such is our Church year, in brief and inadequate outline. It does not seem like much, and in one sense it is not. But I challenge my readers to live the Church year as I have, just for a year, and see the difference it will make in their personal spiritual life. Their lives will be focused the whole year. They will have goals and objectives. Their lives will be lived in expectation, and nothing will be done in vain. Let them give it a try, beginning *now*, for in the wise words of an ancient Chinese proverb,

> All the flowers,
> Of all the tomorrows,
> Are in the seeds of today.